'Twas the night
before Christmas
and all through the house...

© 1985 by Oxmoor House, Inc.
Book Division of Southern Progress Corporation
P.O. Box 2463, Birmingham, Alabama 35201

All designs that appear in this book are the
property of *The Vanessa-Ann Collection*,
Ogden, Utah.

Library of Congress Catalog Number: 84-63034
ISBN: 0-8487-0681-1
Manufactured in the United States of America
First Printing 1985

Executive Editor: Candace Conard Bromberg
Production Manager: Jerry Higdon
Art Director: Bob Nance

All Through The House: Christmas in Cross-Stitch

Editor: Linda Baltzell Wright
Editorial Assistant: Lenda Wyatt
Copy Chief: Mary Jean Haddin
Designer: Diana Smith Morrison
Photographers: Brent Herridge, Courtland Richards
Artist: Janie Farley

To Margaret:

*For yesterday,
   today, and tomorrow . . .
in which you put the strength in
   "together,"
you give more than your part,
you put the hope in tomorrow and
   the joy in our heart.*

Contents

Chapter One
.... 3

Chapter Two
.... 43

Chapter Three
.... 78

Chapter Four
.... 113

Celebrate Christmas with the enduring words of the classic Christmas poem, *The Night Before Christmas*, stitched in the fanciful colors and designs of The Vanessa-Ann Collection. Detailed instructions make it easy for you to complete each project long before the night before Christmas.

All Through the House

SAMPLE

Stitched on light blue Hardanger 22 over two threads, the finished design size is 10⅜" x 13⅜". The fabric was cut 17" x 20". Finished design sizes using other fabrics are Aida 11—10⅜" x 13⅜"; Aida 14—8⅛" x 10½"; Aida 18—6⅜" x 8⅛"; Hardanger 22—5⅛" x 6⅝".

SUSAN BATES

DMC (used for sample)

Step One: Cross-stitch (three strands)

SUSAN BATES		DMC	
1			White
288		445	Lemon-lt.
297		743	Yellow-med.
303		742	Tangerine-lt.
49		3689	Mauve-lt.
49		3689	Mauve-lt. (bead over cross-stitch)
26		957	Geranium-pale
335		606	Orange Red-bright
47		321	Christmas Red
158		775	Baby Blue-lt.
256		704	Chartreuse-bright
239		702	Kelly Green
208		563	Jade-lt.
210		562	Jade-med.
362		437	Tan-lt.
309		435	Brown-vy. lt.
371		433	Brown-med.
397		762	Pearl Grey-vy. lt.
399		452	Shell Grey-med.

Step Two: Backstitch (one strand)

303		742	Tangerine-lt. (angel's harp)
335		606	Orange Red-bright (roof)
147		312	Navy Blue-lt. (trees, angel, snowflakes, snow)
371		433	Brown-med. (all else)

Step Three: French Knots (one strand)

147		312	Navy Blue-lt.

Step Four: Beadwork

Light Blue

1

The stockings were hung by the chimney with care...

Brighten your home for the holidays by making this year a cross-stitch Christmas. Trim the tree with quick-to-stitch cross-stitch wishes. Drape your mantel with a delicate garland of snow-white hearts and doves. Combine your cross-stitch and quilting talents and create colorful patchwork stockings with tiny cross-stitch motifs. Choose from all kinds of wonderful designs that are sure to produce exclamations of delight this Christmas and Christmases to come.

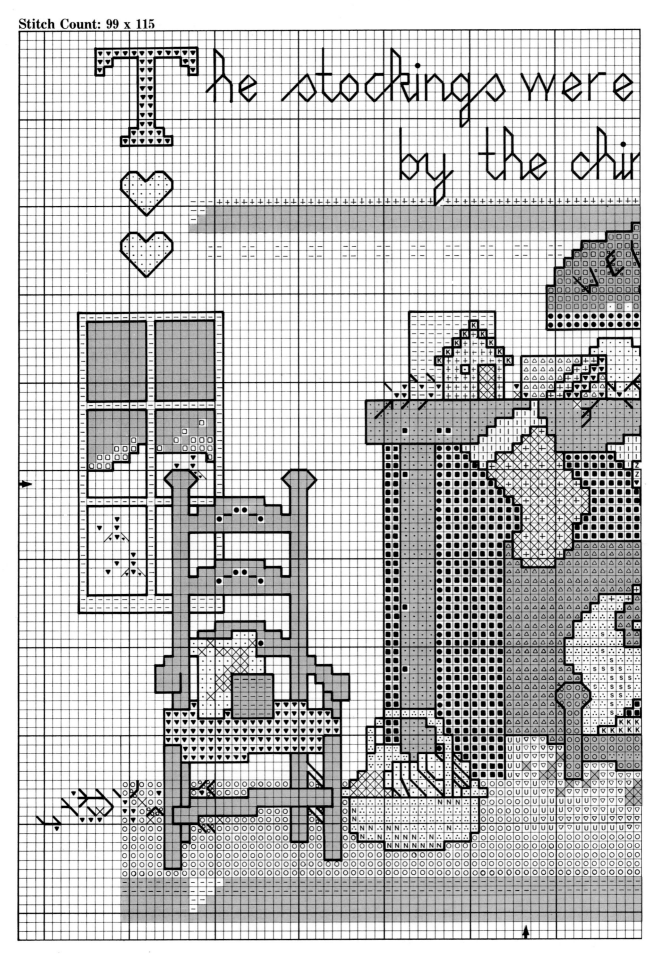

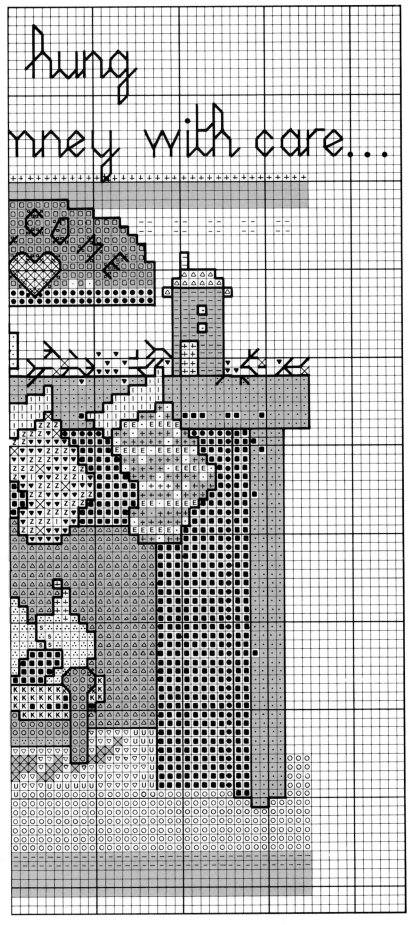

The words of Clement Moore's poem, combined with Trice Boerens's design, create a picture sure to become a family heirloom.

SAMPLE

Stitched on white Linda 27 over two threads, the finished design size is 8½″ x 7⅜″. The fabric was cut 15″ x 14″. The finished design sizes using other fabrics are Aida 11—10½″ x 9″; Aida 14—8¼″ x 7⅛″; Aida 18—6⅜″ x 5½″; Hardanger 22—5¼″ x 4½″.

SUSAN BATES		DMC (used for sample)
		Step One: Cross-stitch (two strands)
1	I	White
295	∴	726 Topaz-lt.
306	N	725 Topaz
298	S	972 Canary-deep
49	·	3689 Mauve-lt.
59	X	326 Rose-vy. deep
108	—	211 Lavender-lt.
101	—	327 Antique Violet-dk.
159		827 Blue-vy. lt.
160	O	813 Blue-lt.
121	∷	793 Cornflower Blue-med.
940	O	792 Cornflower Blue-dk.
849	△	927 Grey Green-med.
206	+	955 Nile Green-lt.
203	E	954 Nile Green
203	O	564 Jade-vy. lt.
188	Z	943 Aquamarine-med.
189	▼	991 Aquamarine-dk.
885	+	739 Tan-ultra vy. lt.
373	·	3045 Yellow Beige-dk.
370	■	434 Brown-lt.
397	U	762 Pearl Grey-vy. lt.
399	O	452 Shell Grey-med.
399	X	451 Shell Grey-dk.
398	▽	415 Pearl Grey-dk.
400	●	414 Steel Grey-dk.
8581	K	646 Beaver Grey-dk.
		Step Two: Backstitch (one strand)
59		326 Rose-vy. deep (yarn in basket)
189		991 Aquamarine-dk. (holly leaves)
401		844 Beaver Grey-ultra dk. (all else)
		Step Three: French Knot (one strand)
401	●	844 Beaver Grey-ultra dk.

Patchwork Stockings

Cross-stitch and quilting, two of the most popular forms of needlework, team up in this colorful trio of stockings. Choose your favorite fabrics and cross-stitch motifs, and each stocking will become a one-of-a-kind design (see photo, page 3).

Heart Alphabet

SAMPLE (page 136)
Stitched on cream Aida 18 with floss that matches stocking fabric. The fabric was cut 5″ x 10″. The total design size of the desired letters should not exceed 7¼″. The letters were centered and spaced two thread units apart.

Tree

SAMPLE
Stitched on cream Aida 18 with floss that matches stocking fabric. The fabric was cut 5″ x 10″. The trees were centered and stitched with each tree spaced three thread units from the next. Finished design sizes using other fabrics are Aida 11—½″ x ⅝″; Aida 14—⅜″ x ½″; Hardanger 22—¼″ x ¼″.

Stitch Count: 5 x 7

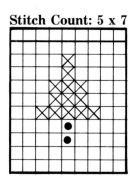

Ho Ho

SAMPLE
Stitched on cream Aida 18 with floss that matches stocking fabric. The fabric was cut 5″ x 10″. The words were centered and stitched vertically, with motifs spaced four thread units apart. Finished design sizes using other fabrics are Aida 11—½″ x 1⅛″; Aida 14—⅜″ x ⅞″; Hardanger 22—¼″ x ⅝″.

Stitch Count: 4 x 13

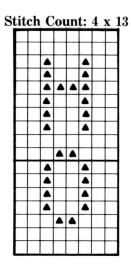

Star

SAMPLE
Stitched on cream Aida 18 with floss that matches stocking fabric. The fabric was cut 5″ x 10″. The stars were centered and stitched, one thread unit apart. Finished design sizes using other fabrics are Aida 11—⅞″ x ⅞″; Aida 14—¾″ x ¾″; Hardanger 22—½″ x ½″.

Stitch Count: 9 x 9

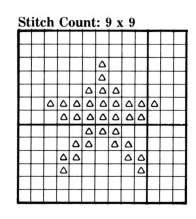

Heart

SAMPLE
Stitched on cream Aida 18 with floss that matches stocking fabric. The fabric was cut 5″ x 10″. The hearts were centered and stitched vertically, with hearts spaced two thread units apart. Finished design sizes using other fabrics are Aida 11—1½″ x 1½″; Aida 14—1¼″ x 1⅛″; Hardanger 22—¾″ x ¾″.

Stitch Count: 17 x 16

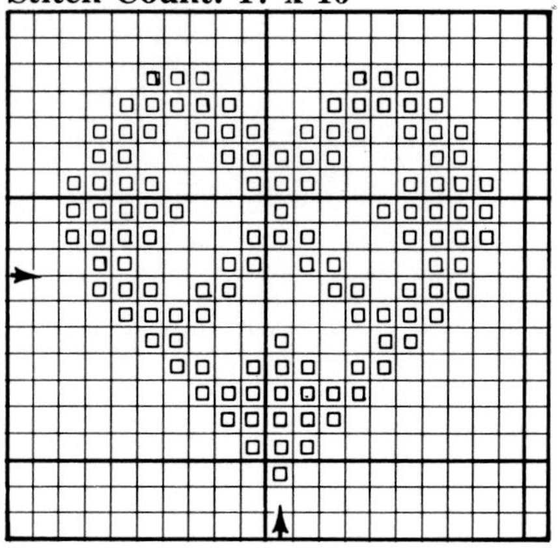

MATERIALS
Three completed cross-stitch designs on Hardanger 22; see sample information
Ruler
Pencil or chalk
Tracing paper for pattern
⅝ yard of 45″-wide print fabric for stocking back and piecing strips
⅝ yard of 45″-wide print fabric for stocking lining and piecing strips
⅝ yard each of two 45″-wide print fabrics for piecing strips
⅝ yard of 45″-wide muslin
Polyester batting
Assorted ½″, 1″, and 2″-wide lace trims and ribbons

DIRECTIONS

1. Transfer the stocking pattern on page 10.

2. From your stitched Hardanger, cut the three piecing strips to the desired sizes, centering each design and adding ¼″ to all the edges for seam allowances.

3. With backing fabric wrong side up, cut one stocking with the toe pointing left.

4. From lining fabric, cut two stockings with toes pointing in opposite directions.

5. Cut two stockings from the muslin and two from the batting.

6. From each of the four print fabrics, cut several strips 2″, 2½″, and 3″ wide by the remaining width of the fabric.

7. On the wrong side of all the piecing strips, mark a ¼″ seam allowance on the top edge. This marked edge becomes the top of each strip.

8. Baste one piece of batting between two muslin stockings. With a pencil or a piece of chalk, mark the toe section with the toe pointing left for the stocking front.

9. Before piecing the stocking front, plan the placement of your Hardanger strips.

OPTION: You may choose to stitch a print piece to a Hardanger piece, to make a strip wide enough to fit across the stocking.

10. To piece the stocking front, place one print strip, right side up, over the muslin foundation, matching the raw edges at the stocking top. Baste the top edge.

11. With right sides together, place a second print strip over the first. Stitch through all the layers. Turn the second print right side up and press. Cut the strip to match the width of the muslin foundation.

12. Repeat this process, varying the widths of the strips and integrating the two Hardanger strips (see photo). To stitch piecing strips at an angle, first stitch one strip to the stocking through all the layers. Then position the seam allowance line of the next strip at the desired angle to the first strip. Stitch on the line through all the layers.

13. To piece the toe section, stitch the remaining Hardanger strip vertically through all the layers over the pencil or chalk line for toe.

14. After the foundation is covered, attach trims and ribbons as desired.

15. Pin lining pieces, right sides together. Stitch, leaving the top edge open and 4″ open above the heel.

16. Baste the remaining batting piece to the wrong side of stocking back piece.

17. Place the front and back of the stocking with right sides together. Stitch, leaving the top edge open. Clip the curved edges and turn right side out.

18. Slide the lining over the stocking with right sides together and side seams matching. Stitch around the top edge. Turn through the 4″ opening in the lining. Slipstitch the opening closed and slip the lining inside the stocking.

19. Cut one 7″ length of 1″-wide lace trim for your loop. Fold it in half and tack the ends inside the stocking at the top of the right side seam.

Stitch Count: 44 x 32

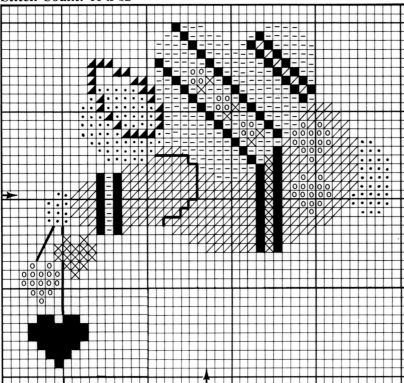

Stitch Count: 24 x 38

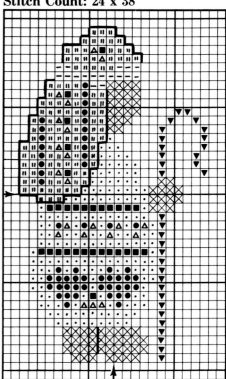

Angel and Shepherd Stockings

Stitch and sew a myriad of hearts to create this romantic pair of stockings. An adorable angel has a large heart for wings, two hearts decorating her gown, and carries two tiny hearts. The charming little shepherd is covered in hearts from head to toe. There are hearts in the beautiful lace edgings. There are even three-dimensional hearts, dangling from satin ribbons.

Stuffed Heart Pattern
seam allowances included

Angel Stocking

SAMPLE
Stitched on cream Aida 18, the finished design size is 2½" x 1⅞". The fabric was cut 10" x 5½". Center and stitch the angel, omitting the large blue heart. Finished design sizes (for one motif) using other fabrics are Aida 11—4" x 3"; Aida 14—3⅛" x 2¼"; Hardanger 22—2" x 1½".

SUSAN BATES		DMC (used for sample)
		Step One: Cross-stitch (three strands)
890	◤	729 Old Gold-med.
832	·	612 Drab Brown-med.
969	╱	316 Antique Mauve-med.
72	–	902 Garnet-vy. dk.
876	✕	502 Blue Green
101	o	327 Antique Violet-dk.
149	■	311 Navy Blue-med.
		Step Two: Backstitch (two strands)
72		902 Garnet-vy. dk.

Shepherd Stocking

SAMPLE
Stitched on cream Aida 18, the finished design size is 8" x 2⅛". The fabric was cut 10" x 5½". The five shepherds were centered and stitched six thread units apart. Finished design sizes using other fabrics are Aida 11—13" x 3½"; Aida 14—10¼" x 2¾"; Hardanger 22—6½" x 1¾".

SUSAN BATES		DMC (used for sample)
		Step One: Cross-stitch (three strands)
849	·	927 Grey Green-med.
869	‖	3042 Antique Violet-lt.
101	△	327 Antique Violet-dk.
44	●	814 Garnet-dk.
901	–	680 Old Gold-dk.
898	✕	611 Drab Brown-dk.
189	■	991 Aquamarine-dk.
401	▼	413 Pewter Grey-dk.
	◣	Gold Metallic (one strand)
		Step Two: Backstitch (two strands)
101		327 Antique Violet-dk. (lettering)
44		814 Garnet-dk. (hat)
401		413 Pewter Grey-dk. (shoes)

8

Monogrammed Band

SAMPLE

Stitched on cream Aida 18 with floss to match fabric color, the fabric was cut 8″ x 5″. For your stocking, choose an evenweave fabric to accommodate the letters of the desired name. Center and stitch the letters using the Heart Alphabet (page 136), spacing the letters two thread units apart.

MATERIALS

Completed cross-stitch design and name on Aida 18; see sample information
Tracing paper for patterns
½ yard of 45″-wide corduroy for stocking; matching thread
½ yard of 45″-wide print fabric for lining
Small pieces of print fabric for hearts; matching thread
⅞ yard of assorted ¼″, ¾″, and 1″-wide cream lace trims; matching thread
16″ of ¼″-wide cream lace trim
3½ yards of ⅛″-wide satin ribbon; matching thread
Polyester batting
Stuffing for hearts

DIRECTIONS

1. Transfer the patterns for the stocking and the heart.

2. From the Aida with the stitched design, cut one 8″ x 3¼″ piece with the design centered. From the Aida with the stitched name, cut one 6″ x 1¾″ piece with the name centered. Zigzag the edges of both pieces to prevent raveling.

3. With toes pointing in opposite directions, cut two stockings from the corduroy and two from the print fabric used for the lining.

4. From the polyester batting fabric, cut two stockings.

5. From the print fabric cut two hearts for each stuffed heart you desire.

6. Baste the Aida with the design 2¾″ below the top edge of the corduroy stocking with the toe pointing left. Baste the Aida with the name 2¼″ from the edge of the toe (see photo, page 9). Stitch the Aida pieces with cream thread.

7. Cut two 6″ lengths of lace trim to border the Aida with the name. Stitch the trim to each side of the Aida through all the layers.

8. Cut two 8″ lengths of lace trim to border the Aida with the design. Stitch the trim to each side of the Aida through the layers.

9. Pin the lining pieces with right sides together. Stitch, leaving the top edge open and a 4″ opening above the heel.

10. Baste the batting to the wrong side of the corduroy stockings.

11. Stitch the right sides of the stocking front and back together, leaving the top edge open. Turn right side out.

12. With the right sides of the lining and stocking together, slide the lining over the stocking, matching the side seams. Stitch around the top edge and turn through the 4″ opening in the lining. Slipstitch the opening closed and slip the lining inside the stocking.

13. Pin a 16″ length of the ¼″-wide cream lace trim around the top edge of stocking ⅛″ above the border of the Aida design, and slipstitch in place.

14. Stitch the hearts with right sides together, leaving a 1″ opening. Turn right side out and stuff. Slipstitch the opening closed. Repeat for the remaining hearts.

15. Cut two 5″ lengths of ribbon. To make a loop to hang the stocking, fold both lengths in half and tack the ends inside the stocking on the right side. Cut the remaining ribbon into six equal lengths. Handling all the lengths as one, tie them tightly into a bow. Attach the bow securely to the upper left seam.

16. Attach the hearts to the ribbons (see photo, page 9).

A

B

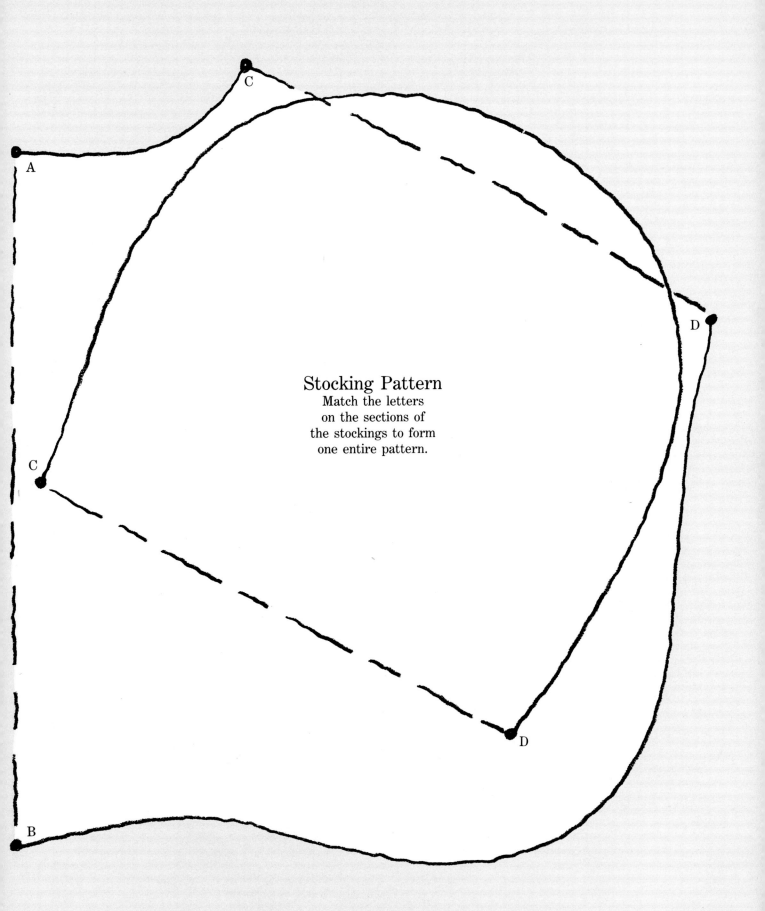

Stocking Pattern
Match the letters
on the sections of
the stockings to form
one entire pattern.

Blue Velvet Stocking

Seasonal cross-stitch designs and shiny satin ribbons decorate this luxurious blue velvet stocking. The color blue is a surprisingly successful alternative to the traditional Christmas colors.

SAMPLE

Stitched on white Linda 27 over two threads, the finished design size for the stocking is 6⅝" x 2". The fabric was cut 10" x 5". The tree, goose, and ornament motifs were centered and stitched ⅜" apart.

Stitch Count: 27 x 27

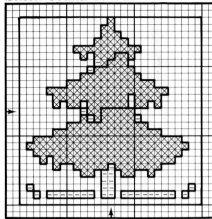
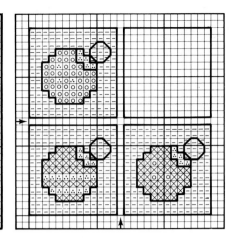
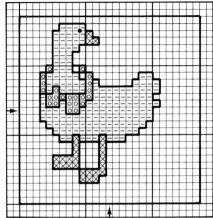

FINISHING INSTRUCTIONS

Tree Motif: Small red beads are stitched randomly, as ornaments on a tree.

Ornament Motif: Small red beads are stitched over the red cross-stitches on one of the green ornaments, and small white beads are stitched over the white cross-stitches on the red ornament.

Goose Motif: Small red beads are stitched over the wreath around the goose's neck. A small bow tied with the ¹⁄₁₆″-wide red satin ribbon is tacked to the wreath.

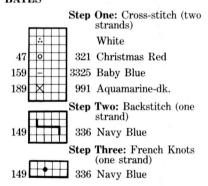

SUSAN BATES		DMC (used for sample)
		Step One: Cross-stitch (two strands)
		White
47	o	321 Christmas Red
159	–	3325 Baby Blue
189	☒	991 Aquamarine-dk.
		Step Two: Backstitch (one strand)
149		336 Navy Blue
		Step Three: French Knots (one strand)
149	•	336 Navy Blue

MATERIALS

Completed cross-stitch on white Linda; see sample information
Tracing paper for pattern
½ yard of 45″-wide blue velvet for stocking; matching thread
½ yard of 45″-wide print fabric for lining

2 yards of ½″-wide blue satin ribbon; matching thread
1½ yards of ¼″-wide red satin ribbon; matching thread
1 yard of ⅛″-wide green satin ribbon; matching thread
White thread
Polyester batting

DIRECTIONS

1. Transfer the pattern for the stocking on page 10.

2. From the white Linda, cut one 8″ x 3″ piece making sure the design is centered. Zigzag all edges.

3. From the velvet, cut two stockings with toes pointing in opposite directions.

4. From the print fabric used for the lining, cut two stockings that are opposite.

5. Cut two stockings from the polyester batting.

6. Baste the Linda 2¾″ below the top edge of the stocking with the toe pointing right. Stitch both long edges using matching thread.

7. Cut three 8″ lengths of the blue ribbon. Slipstitch two ribbon lengths to the stocking on each side of the Linda, overlapping the Linda ¼″. Slipstitch the third ribbon length to the stocking 1½″ below the top edge.

8. Cut one 8″ length of red ribbon and two 8″ lengths of green ribbon. Center and slipstitch the red ribbon between the top two blue ribbons on the stocking. Slipstitch the green ribbon lengths on each side of the red ribbon (see photo).

9. Cut two 6″ lengths of blue and green ribbons. Also cut one 6″ length of red ribbon. Slipstitch one blue ribbon length across the stocking 1½″ from the edge of the toe (see photo). Stitch the second blue ribbon length 2¾″ from the edge of the toe. Center and slipstitch the red ribbon between the two blue ribbon lengths. Slipstitch the two green ribbon lengths on each side of the red ribbon.

10. Complete Steps 9 through 12 of the Angel and Shepherd Stockings (page 10).

11. Cut one 5½″ length of red ribbon. To make a loop for hanging the stocking, fold the ribbon in half and tack the ribbon ends inside the stocking on the left side.

12. Handling the remaining blue and red ribbons as one, tie a bow and tack it to the blue ribbon on the bottom edge of the Linda strip.

Miniature Mittens

Miniature mittens make adorable Christmas ornaments to give your children. Cross-stitch the child's name and birthdate on one mitten and a favorite motif on the other. The goose motif used here was taken from the graph for the Blue Velvet Stocking on page 93.

SAMPLE

Stitched on Cracked Wheat Ragusa 14 over one thread, the finished design size for the goose is 1⅞" x 1⅞". The fabric was cut 6" x 6". A small bow was tied with the ⅟₁₆"-wide red satin ribbon and tacked to the wreath around the goose's neck. Finished design sizes for other fabrics are Aida 11—2½" x 2½"; Aida 14—1⅞" x 1⅞"; Aida 18—1½" x 1½"; Hardanger 22—1¼" x 1¼".

MATERIALS

Completed cross-stitch for two mittens on Cracked Wheat Ragusa; see sample information

Tracing paper for pattern

Two 5" x 6" pieces of unstitched Cracked Wheat Ragusa; matching thread

10" of ⅛"-wide blue satin ribbon; matching thread

Stuffing

14

Clockwise from the top: Ruffled Pillow, Christmas Wishes, Envelope Pillow, Monogrammed Sachets, Miniature Mittens.

DIRECTIONS

1. Transfer the mitten pattern.

2. From the stitched Cracked Wheat Ragusa, cut two opposite mittens with the designs centered on each. Zigzag the edges to keep them from raveling.

3. From the unstitched pieces of Cracked Wheat Ragusa, cut two opposite mittens and zigzag the edges.

4. With the right sides of one stitched and one unstitched mitten together, sew the edges, leaving the bottom edge open. Carefully clip the seam allowances around thumb. Turn right side out. Stuff the mitten and slipstitch the opening closed. Sew a running stitch ½″ from the bottom edge across the mitten. Gather this slightly and secure the thread.

5. Repeat the same steps for the second mitten. Tack the blue ribbon to the side seam opposite the thumb.

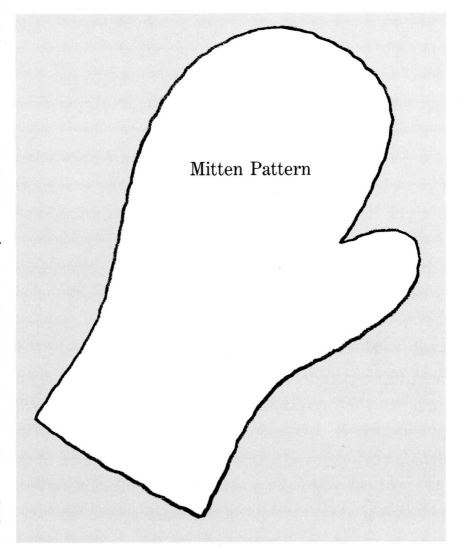

Mitten Pattern

Monogrammed Sachets

Monogram a gift, and it becomes even more special. These ornaments and sachets are so quick and easy, you can stitch one for everybody on your Christmas list.

SAMPLE
Stitched on cream Aida 14, with floss to match the color of the backing fabric. The fabric was cut 6″ x 6″. The letters were centered and stitched using the Heart Alphabet on page 136.

MATERIALS
Completed cross-stitch on cream
  Aida 14; see sample information
Small piece of colored fabric;
  matching thread
½ yard small cording
Assorted trims, laces, ribbons
Stuffing
Small amount of potpourri

DIRECTIONS
1. From the Aida, cut one 4″ square with the initial centered.

2. From the fabric, cut one 4″ square. Cut 1¼″-wide bias strips, piecing as needed to equal 15″. Cover the cording.

3. Place the cording on the right side of the Aida, with the raw edges matching. Stitch on the stitching line of the cording.

4. With the right sides of the Aida and the fabric piece together, stitch again on the stitching line of the cording, leaving a 1½″ opening on one side. Clip the corners and turn right side out.

5. Stuff firmly (potpourri may be added now), and slipstitch the opening closed.

6. Add lace, trim, or ribbons as desired. Fold one length of ribbon in half for a loop to hang the ornament, and tack the ends to the upper left corner on back of the ornament.

Treetop Star

You don't even have to thread a needle to complete this project. Cut out three stars from perforated paper, put them together, and glue on lots of tiny little beads to make the star sparkle.

MATERIALS

Tracing paper for pattern
Three pieces of 9″ x 12″ cream perforated paper
15 dozen small beads, assorted colors
Tacky glue
6 yards of 1/8″-wide red satin ribbon

DIRECTIONS

1. Transfer the pattern for the star; include all the information. Trace the star onto the perforated paper three times. Cut out the stars, noting the inside cutting lines.

2. Glue the beads, about 1″ apart, to both sides of all three stars.

3. Cut the ribbon into six 1-yard lengths. Glue the ribbon to both sides of the edge of each star, folding the ribbon at the corners.

4. Place together the two stars that are slit at the bottom. Slide the third star that is slit from the point over the other two.

5. Glue the seams together.

For two stars cut on this line.

For one star cut on this line.

Treetop Star Pattern

Clockwise from the top: Treetop Star, Angel Candle Ring, Dove Garland, Christmas Wishes, Envelope Pillow, Dove Tree Skirt, Dove Wrap, Blue Velvet Stocking, Season's Greetings, Angel Pinafore, Goose Collar, Family Sampler, Gift Bag, Snowman Pillow, Soft-sculpture Dove.

Stitch Count: 58 x 18

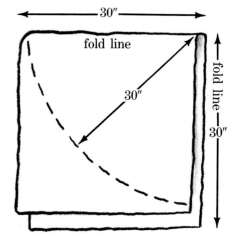

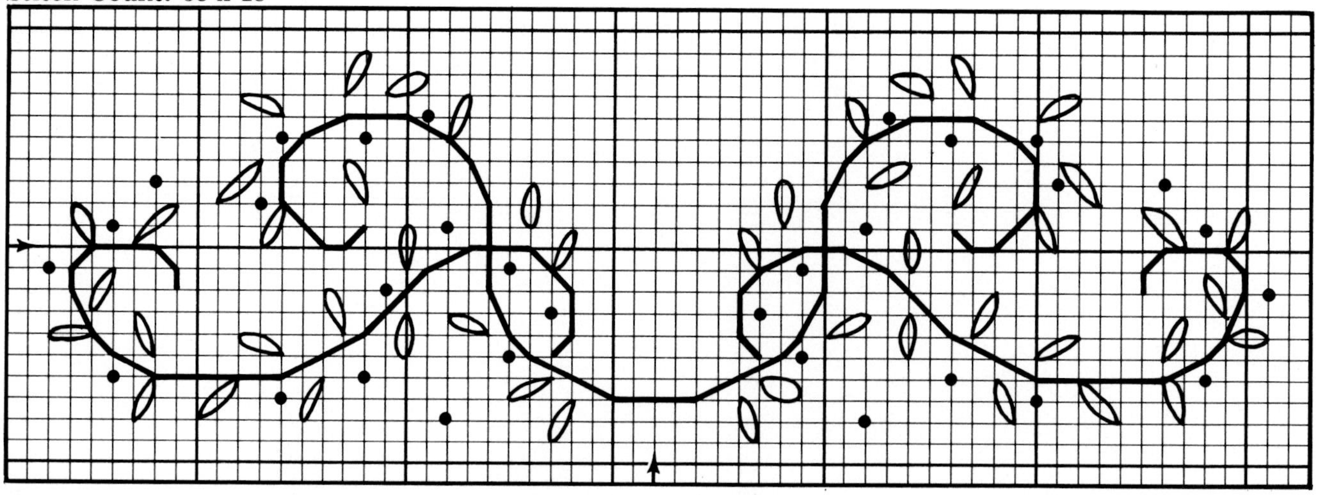

Doves of Peace

Why not carry out one theme when decorating your home this Christmas season? Tie the ribbons of the doves and hearts together and make a garland for your mantel. Sew hearts and doves to a skirt for your tree. Wrap single doves around throw pillows for your sofa and sew soft-sculpture doves to make a centerpiece. Of course, not all these projects need to be made this year. Choose one now and save the others for Christmases to come (see photo, page 16).

SAMPLES

Stitched on white Linda 27 over two threads, the finished design size is 4¼" x 1⅜. The dove pattern was traced onto the fabric, and the placement of the stitching was marked using a dressmaker's pen. Finished design sizes for other fabrics are Aida 11—5¼" x 1⅝"; Aida 14—4⅛" x 1¼"; Aida 18—3¼" x 1"; Hardanger 22—2⅝" x ⅞".

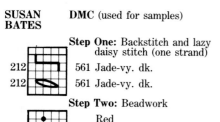

SUSAN BATES   **DMC** (used for samples)

Step One: Backstitch and lazy daisy stitch (one strand)

212	561 Jade-vy. dk.
212	561 Jade-vy. dk.

Step Two: Beadwork
Red

Dove Tree Skirt

MATERIALS

Completed cross-stitch with beads for six doves (three doves facing right and three doves facing left) on white Linda; see sample information
Tracing paper for patterns
Dressmaker's pen
Dressmaker's chalk
Large-eyed needle
Small pieces of unstitched white Linda for three hearts; matching thread
3¾ yards of 60"-wide green fabric; matching thread
3 yards of 45"-wide polyester fleece
¾ yard of 45"-wide cranberry chintz for binding; matching thread
Fusing material
3 yards of ⅛"-wide cranberry satin ribbon for bows
2½ yards of ½"-wide green satin ribbon for ties
½ yard of ⅜"-wide pink satin ribbon for roses; matching thread
⅝ yard of ⅜"-wide cranberry satin ribbon for roses
¼ yard of ⅜"-wide green satin ribbon for leaves
10" of 1/16"-wide pink satin ribbon

DIRECTIONS

1. Transfer the patterns for the dove and the heart on page 20.

2. Trace three hearts on the unstitched Linda, using a dressmaker's pen.

3. Fold the green fabric into a large square about 60" x 60". Cut the fabric on the fold to make two equal square pieces.

4. Fold one square into quarters making about a 30" square. Pin securely through all the layers. Measure 30" from the center fold and mark (Diagram 1). Cut on the marked arc through all the layers.

Diagram 1

5. With the fabric still pinned securely, measure 4" from the center fold and mark. Cut on the marked arc through all layers.

6. Cut from the outside edge to the edge of the smaller circle on one fold line. This cut becomes the center back opening (Diagram 2).

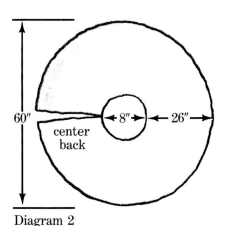

Diagram 2

7. Place the tree skirt over the remaining 60″ x 60″ square and cut out a second skirt.

8. Cut one tree skirt from fleece, piecing as needed.

9. Cut 1½″-wide bias strips from the cranberry chintz, piecing as needed to equal 5¼ yds.

10. Trim the ¼″ seam allowance from the dove and heart pattern. From the fusing material cut six doves (three doves facing right and three doves facing left) and three hearts.

11. Designate one green tree skirt as the top. Begin at the center back opening of the skirt and mark five 37½″ intervals on the outside edge. Then beginning at the center back of the inside edge mark five 5″ intervals. Using dressmaker's chalk, connect the marks at the inside edge to the outside edge to separate the five areas. Also, mark the center of each of the five sections 3″ from the outside edge.

12. Center and pin one heart cut from the fusing material to the wrong side of one heart traced onto the Linda. Place the heart in the center front section, with the tip of the heart on the mark that is 3″ from

the bottom edge. Fuse according to manufacturer's instructions and cut away excess fabric.

13. Center and pin one dove cut from the fusing material to the wrong side of one dove traced onto the Linda. Place the breast of the bird 2″ from the heart, with the bottom edge of the dove on the 3″ mark, and fuse. Cut away any excess fabric. Add a second dove on the other side of the heart (Diagram 3).

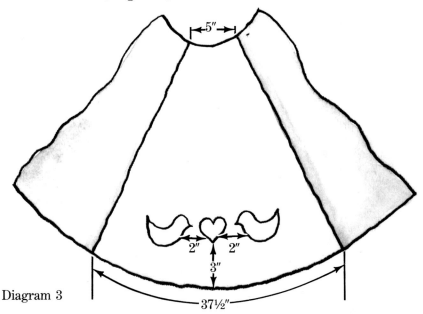

Diagram 3

14. Fuse the remaining hearts and doves to complete the three front sections of the skirt.

15. With white thread, satin-stitch over the pen lines of all the hearts and doves. Trim excess Linda fabric and satin-stitch again.

16. Complete Steps 7 through 9 of the Dove Garland (page 22). Make two cranberry ribbon roses and one pink ribbon rose for two hearts, and two pink ribbon roses and one cranberry ribbon rose for the other heart.

17. Thread an 18″ length of ⅛″-wide cranberry ribbon onto a large-eyed needle. Working from the front of the tree skirt, thread the ribbon behind the dove's neck. Tie it into a bow and trim the ends. Repeat for the remaining doves.

18. Baste the fleece to the wrong side of the tree skirt top.

19. With right sides together, match and pin both layers of the green fabric together. Stitch along the center back edge, the inside edge, and the second center back edge, but leave the bottom edge open. Trim the corners and clip the seam allowance around the inside edge. Turn the tree skirt right side out and baste the entire unit.

20. Topstitch 1″ from the seamline around the inside edge and on the chalk lines separating the five sections. Also stitch around each heart.

21. Stitch the right sides of the bias strip and tree skirt top together. Trim any excess fleece. Fold the bias strip in half and then to the back of the skirt; whipstitch in place.

22. For the position of the ribbon ties, mark both edges of the center back opening 1″, 12″, and 23″ from the inside edge.

23. Cut the ½″-wide green satin ribbon into six 15″ lengths. Fold one end of each length back twice to the wrong side of the ribbon. Tack it securely to the edge of the opening at the marks. Repeat this step to make three sets of ties.

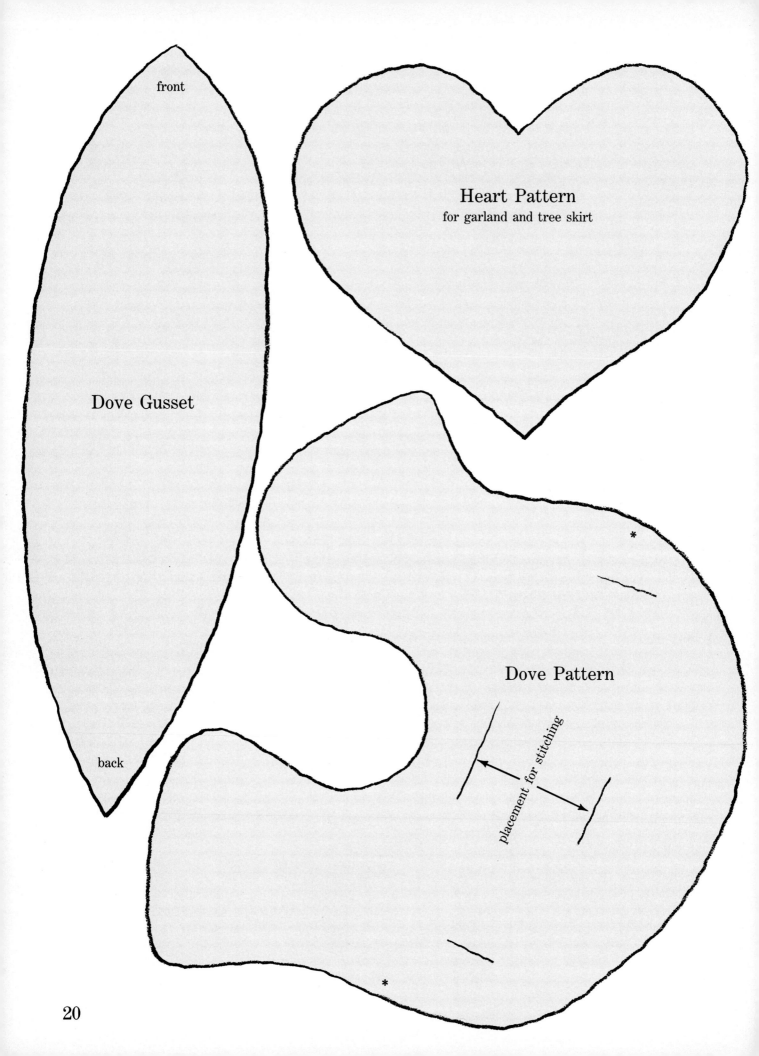

front

Heart Pattern
for garland and tree skirt

Dove Gusset

back

Dove Pattern

placement for stitching

*

*

20

Soft-Sculpture Dove

MATERIALS

Completed cross-stitch with beads on white Linda; see sample information

Tracing paper for patterns

10″ square piece of unstitched white Linda; matching thread

Stuffing

12″ of ¹⁄₁₆″-wide cranberry ribbon

DIRECTIONS

1. Transfer the patterns for the dove and the dove gusset.

2. From the stitched Linda cut one dove. Zigzag the edges.

3. From the unstitched Linda, cut one dove for the back and one gusset piece for the bottom. Zigzag the edges.

4. With right sides of the front and back of the dove together, stitch around the top of the dove between the stars (see pattern); backstitch.

5. With right sides together, stitch one side of the gusset piece to the dove front as indicated on the pattern. Repeat on the second side, leaving a 2½″ opening. Turn right side out.

6. Stuff the dove until it is firm; then slipstitch the opening closed.

7. Tie the cranberry ribbon in a bow around the dove's neck.

21

Dove Garland

MATERIALS (for two doves and one heart)

Completed cross-stitch with beads for two doves on white Linda; see sample information

Tracing paper for patterns

⅜ yard of 45″-wide unstitched white Linda; matching thread

Polyester fleece

¼ yard of ⅜″-wide pink satin ribbon for roses; matching thread

⅛ yard of ⅜″-wide cranberry satin ribbon for roses; matching thread

⅛ yard of ⅜″-wide green satin ribbon for leaf; matching thread

10″ of 1/16″-wide pink satin ribbon

1 yard of ¼″-wide picot-edge pink satin ribbon

2½ yards of ¼″-wide green satin ribbon

DIRECTIONS

1. Transfer the patterns for the dove and the heart on page 20.

2. Position the pattern for the dove over the stitched design as indicated on the pattern. Cut one dove with the head pointing left and one dove with the head pointing right.

3. Cut two doves and two hearts from the unstitched Linda.

4. Cut two doves and one heart from the fleece.

5. Layer the fleece between the wrong sides of the unstitched Linda and the design piece and pin. Satin-stitch on the pen line. Trim close to the stitching and satin-stitch a second time over the first stitching.

6. Layer the fleece between two Linda hearts, and baste together. Using white thread, satin-stitch over the edges; trim and stitch again.

7. Make two ribbon roses from the ⅜″-wide pink ribbon and one ribbon rose from the ⅜″-wide cranberry ribbon. For each rose, place a 3″ or 4″ length of ribbon wrong side up on a flat surface. Fold both ends at a right angle to the ribbon. Hand-stitch a gathering thread across the bottom edge, leaving the needle threaded (Diagram 1). As you slightly gather the ribbon, wrap it to make a flower (Diagram 2). Force the needle through the lower edge of the ribbon and secure the thread. Trim any excess ribbon.

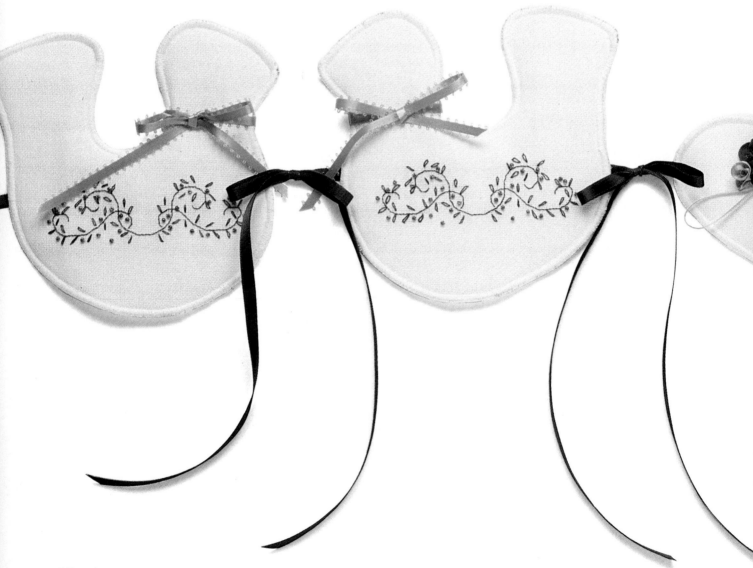

22

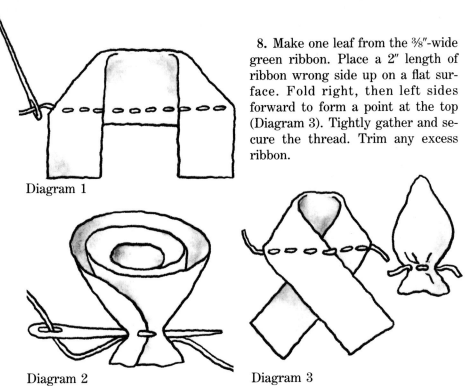

Diagram 1

Diagram 2

Diagram 3

8. Make one leaf from the ⅜″-wide green ribbon. Place a 2″ length of ribbon wrong side up on a flat surface. Fold right, then left sides forward to form a point at the top (Diagram 3). Tightly gather and secure the thread. Trim any excess ribbon.

9. Attach the two roses and the leaf to the top of the heart, just left of the center. Tie a 10″ length of the ¹⁄₁₆″-wide ribbon in a bow and attach it below the roses.

10. Cut a ¼″-wide pink satin ribbon into two equal lengths. Tie a bow around the necks of both doves.

11. Cut a ¼″-wide green satin ribbon into six equal lengths. Sew one end of two ribbons to the center of the backs of the doves and the heart.

12. Tie the heart between the two doves to form a garland. Continue to add more doves and hearts until your garland is the length desired.

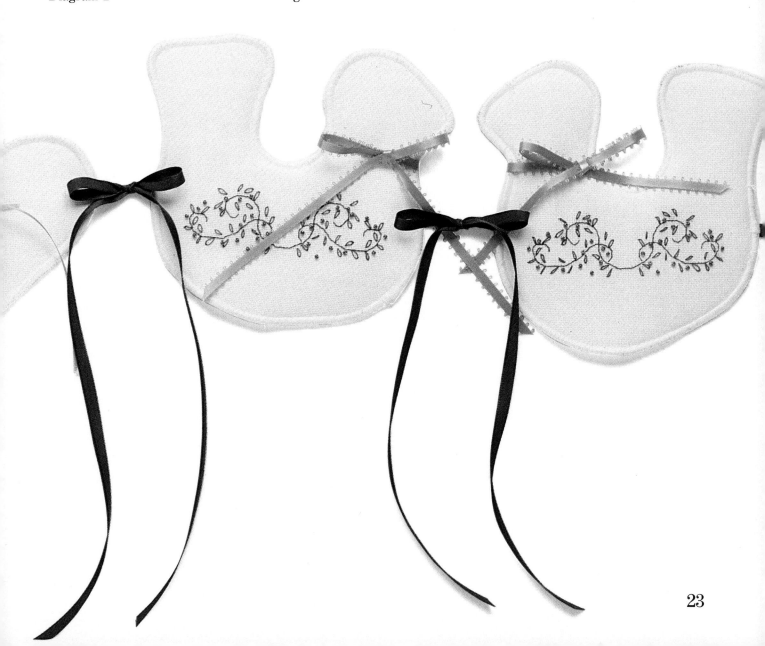

Dove Wrap

MATERIALS
Completed cross-stitch with beads on white Linda; see sample information
Tracing paper for pattern
Dressmaker's pen
10″ square of unstitched white Linda; matching thread
⅜ yard of 45″-wide green fabric for pillow; matching thread
1¼ yards of small cording
Polyester fleece
1½ yards of ¼″-wide cranberry satin ribbon; matching thread
½ yard of ¼″-wide picot-edge pink satin ribbon
Stuffing

DIRECTIONS
1. Transfer the pattern for the dove on page 20. Position the pattern over the stitched design as indicated on the pattern. Trace the dove onto the Linda fabric with a dressmaker's pen.

2. From the green fabric, cut two 11″ squares for the pillow. To cover the cording, cut 1¼″-wide bias strips, piecing as needed to equal 1¼ yards.

3. From the fleece, cut one dove.

4. Stitch the covered cording to the right side of one 11″ x 11″ green fabric piece.

5. With the right sides of both 11″ square green pieces together, stitch on the stitching line of the cording, leaving a 5″ opening on one side. Turn the pillow right side out and stuff. Slipstitch the opening closed.

6. Tuck each corner inside ¾″ and tack the cording together to form square corners.

7. Layer the fleece between the wrong sides of the unstitched Linda and the design piece, and pin. Satin-stitch on the pen line. Trim close to the satin stitching and satin-stitch a second time over the first stitching.

8. Tie a pink ribbon in a bow around the dove's neck.

9. Cut the cranberry ribbon into four equal lengths. Attach one ribbon length on each side of the back of the dove. Attach one end of each ribbon length to the center of each side of the pillow front.

10. Tie the dove to the pillow (see photo).

Angel Candle Ring

These funny little dancing angels were borrowed from the graph for the Angel Pinafore in Chapter 2. Cross-stitching a single motif or a section of a graph can create an entirely new design look (see photo, page 16).

SAMPLE
Stitched on white Aida 14. Compare finished design size of desired motifs with the circumference of your candle. The fabric was cut 7½″ x candle's circumference plus 2″. The motifs were centered vertically and repeated as desired. Finished design sizes for other fabrics are Aida 11—8⅛″ x 9⅜″; Aida 14—6⅜″ x 7⅜″; Aida 18—5″ x 5¾″; Hardanger 22—4″ x 4⅝″.

SUSAN BATES		DMC (used for sample)	
Step One: Cross-stitch (two strands)			
1			White
386		746	Off-White
288		445	Lemon-lt.
778		754	Peach Flesh-lt.
24		776	Pink-med.
105		209	Lavender-dk.
167		519	Sky Blue
264		772	Pine Green-lt.
206		955	Nile Green-lt.
942		738	Tan-vy. lt.
914		3064	Sportsman Flesh-med.
Step Two: Backstitch (one strand)			
380		839	Beige Brown-dk.
Step Three: French Knots (one strand)			
380		839	Beige Brown-dk.

MATERIALS
Completed cross-stitch on white Aida; see sample information
White thread

DIRECTIONS
1. With the design centered, cut the Aida 7″ x candle's circumference plus 2″.

2. Press 2″ of the bottom edge of the Aida to the wrong side.

3. Press 2¼″ of the top edge of the Aida to the wrong side. Turn under ½″ and slipstitch. Fold the raw ends of the strip to the inside.

4. Place the Aida band around the candle. Insert one end of the strip inside the opposite end until the strip is tight around the candle; then slipstitch.

Patchwork Stars

Gather together your scraps of calico, cross-stitch fabrics and ribbons to create stars for your tree or windows (see photo, page 26).

SAMPLE
Stitched on cream Aida 18 with floss to match fabric color, the finished design size is ½″ x 1⅝″. The fabric for each cross-stitch section was cut 4″ x 5″. Three stars were centered and stitched vertically, with the stars spaced one thread unit apart. Finished design sizes for other fabrics are Aida 11—⅞″ x ⅞″; Aida 14—¾″ x ¾″; Hardanger 22—½″ x ½″.

MATERIALS
Three pieces of completed cross-stitch on cream Aida; see sample information
Tracing paper for pattern
Small pieces of print fabric; matching thread
1 yard of 1/16″-wide braid
Stuffing

DIRECTIONS
1. Transfer the pattern for the star.

2. From the Aida, cut three star pieces with the designs centered.

Stitch Count: 49 x 23

3. From the print fabric, cut nine star pieces.

4. Lay out the six sections for the ornament front, alternating the Aida and print pieces. With the right sides together, stitch three pieces for the upper half of the star. Stitch the other three pieces for the lower half of star. Then with right sides together and centers matched, stitch the two halves to one another.

5. For the ornament back, repeat Step 4 with the remaining print pieces.

6. With the right sides together, match the front and back of the star at each point. Stitch around the outside edge, leaving the side of one point open. Clip the corners. Turn right side out, making sure that each point is sharp.

Stitch Count: 9 x 9

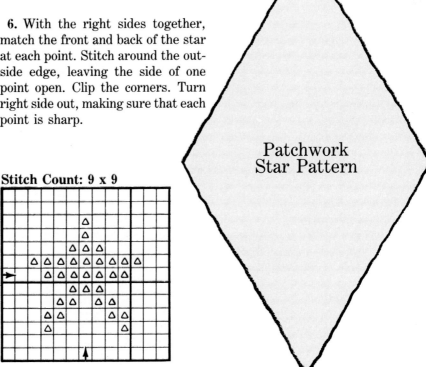

7. Stuff the star and slipstitch the opening closed. Tack the ornament front and back together at the center point of the star.

8. Cover the seam lines of the star with braid, tacking the braid in place (see photo). Tie a small bow with the remaining braid and tack it to the center front of the ornament.

Patchwork
Star Pattern

Patchwork Hearts

Piece a row of little cross-stitched hearts between strips of calico, and then sew the strips together to form a larger patchwork heart. If you turn some of the strips of fabric wrong side out, you can create a subtle contrast in color.

SAMPLE

Stitched on cream Aida 18 with floss to match the fabric color, the finished design size is 5¼" x ⅞". The fabric was cut 8" x 4". The five hearts were centered horizontally and spaced two thread units apart. Finished heart sizes for other fabrics are Aida 11—1½" x 1½"; Aida 14—1¼" x 1⅛"; Hardanger 22—¾" x ¾".

MATERIALS

Completed cross-stitch on cream
 Aida 18; see sample information
Tracing paper for pattern
One 7" square piece of print fabric
 for back
Small pieces of assorted print fab-
 rics; matching thread
Stuffing

Stitch Count: 17 x 16

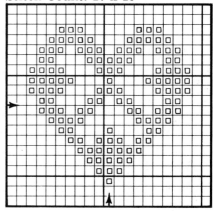

Clockwise from the top: Stephanie's First Christmas, Patchwork Stars, Patchwork Hearts, Christmas Wreath Pillow.

continued

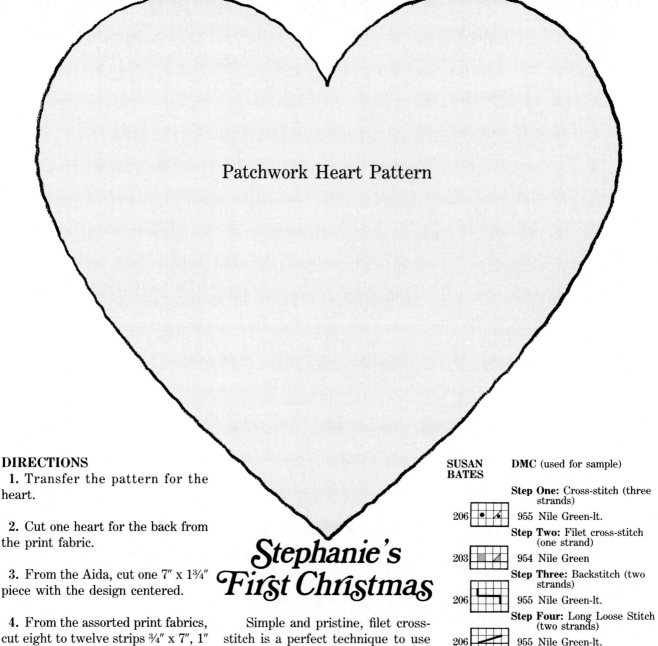

Patchwork Heart Pattern

DIRECTIONS

1. Transfer the pattern for the heart.

2. Cut one heart for the back from the print fabric.

3. From the Aida, cut one 7″ x 1¾″ piece with the design centered.

4. From the assorted print fabrics, cut eight to twelve strips ¾″ x 7″, 1″ x 7″ and 1¼″ x 7″. The number and size of strips used will be determined by individual preference.

5. With the right sides together, stitch the assorted print strips and Aida strip together to make a 7″ square; press.

6. Place the heart pattern diagonally over the pieced front. Cut out one heart for the ornament front.

7. Stitch with the right sides of the ornament front and back together, leaving a 2″ opening on the side. Clip the curved edges and turn right side out. Stuff the ornament and slipstitch the opening closed.

Stephanie's First Christmas

Simple and pristine, filet cross-stitch is a perfect technique to use when working a design for baby. A silhouette dominates the design in this needlework, and the background is usually stitched in one color (see photo, page 26).

SAMPLE

Stitched on Christmas green Hardanger 22 over two threads, the finished design size is 8⅛″ x 9⅛″. The fabric was cut 14″ x 15″. Finished design sizes for other fabrics are Aida 11—8⅛″ x 9⅛″; Aida 14—6⅜″ x 7¼″; Aida 18—5″ x 5⅝″; Hardanger 22—4⅛″ x 4⅝″.
Also needed: One 5″ length of ¹⁄₁₆″-wide red satin ribbon; matching thread.

SUSAN BATES		DMC (used for sample)
		Step One: Cross-stitch (three strands)
206		955 Nile Green-lt.
		Step Two: Filet cross-stitch (one strand)
203		954 Nile Green
		Step Three: Backstitch (two strands)
206		955 Nile Green-lt.
		Step Four: Long Loose Stitch (two strands)
206		955 Nile Green-lt.
		Step Five: Beadwork
		Red

Tie the ribbon in a small bow and tack it to the wreath (see photo, page 26).

MATERIALS

Completed cross-stitch on green Hardanger; see sample information
⅜ yard of 45″-wide unstitched green Hardanger; matching thread
1½ yards of medium cording
3 yards of ¹⁄₁₆″-wide red satin ribbon
Large-eyed needle
Stuffing

Stitch Count: 90 x 101

DIRECTIONS

1. From the stitched Hardanger, cut one 12″ x 13″ piece with the design centered for the pillow front.

2. For the pillow back, cut one 12″ x 13″ piece from the unstitched Hardanger. Also cut 2″-wide bias strips, piecing as needed, to equal 1½ yards. Cover the cording.

3. Using a zipper foot on your machine, stitch the cording to the right side of the pillow front.

4. With right sides together, stitch the pillow front to the back on the stitching line of the cording. Leave a 5″ opening on one side and turn. Stuff and slipstitch the opening closed.

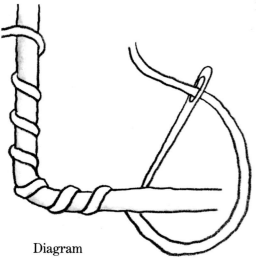

Diagram

5. Mark ½″ intervals on the cording with pins. Thread the ribbon through the large-eyed needle. Beginning at the bottom of the pillow, spiral the ribbon around the cording at the marked intervals (Diagram).

Christmas Wreath Pillow

For color and charm, add hearts and daisies to a traditional evergreen wreath, to frame these Christmas toys and treasures (see photo, page 26).

SAMPLE

Stitched on white Hardanger 22 over two threads, finished design size is 7″ x 6¾″. The fabric was cut 10″ x 10″. Finished design sizes for other fabrics are Aida 11—7″ x 6¾″; Aida 14—5½″ x 5¼″; Aida 18—4¼″ x 4⅛″; Hardanger 22—3½″ x 3⅜″.

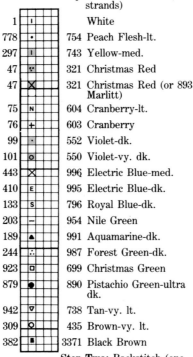

SUSAN BATES		DMC (used for sample)
		Step One: Cross-stitch (three strands)
1	I	White
778	•	754 Peach Flesh-lt.
297	I	743 Yellow-med.
47	⊡	321 Christmas Red
47	X	321 Christmas Red (or 893 Marlitt)
75	N	604 Cranberry-lt.
76	+	603 Cranberry
99	·	552 Violet-dk.
101	o	550 Violet-vy. dk.
443	X	996 Electric Blue-med.
410	E	995 Electric Blue-dk.
133	s	796 Royal Blue-dk.
203	–	954 Nile Green
189	▲	991 Aquamarine-dk.
244	∴	987 Forest Green-dk.
923	□	699 Christmas Green
879	●	890 Pistachio Green-ultra dk.
942	▽	738 Tan-vy. lt.
309	◑	435 Brown-vy. lt.
382	■	3371 Black Brown
		Step Two: Backstitch (one strand)
879		890 Pistachio Green-ultra dk. (flowers)
382		3371 Black Brown (all else)
		Step Three: French Knots (one strand)
382	•	3371 Black Brown
		Step Four: Smyrna Cross (three strands)
316	✳	970 Pumpkin-lt.

MATERIALS

Completed cross-stitch on white Hardanger; see sample information
½ yard of 45″-wide dark green fabric; matching thread
¼ yard of 45″-wide burgundy fabric; matching thread
18″ x 18″ pillow form

DIRECTIONS

1. For the pillow front, cut one 8½″ square from the stitched Hardanger with the design centered.

2. For the pillow back, cut one 16½″ square from the dark green fabric. Also cut four 3″ x 14½″ strips for the outside border.

3. From the burgundy fabric, cut four 3″ x 10½″ strips for the inside border.

4. With right sides together, match the raw edges of one burgundy strip to the top edge of the Hardanger and stitch. Cut off the excess fabric from the right edge (Diagram 1). Turn the border strip right side up and press the seam toward the darker fabric.

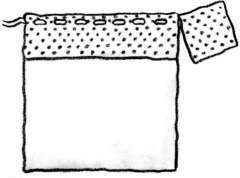

Diagram 1

5. With right sides together, match the raw edges of the second burgundy strip to the left edge of the Hardanger and across the first burgundy strip. Stitch this border strip to the Hardanger and the first border strip. (Diagram 2). Then turn the border right side up and press the seam toward the darker fabric.

Stitch Count: 77 x 74

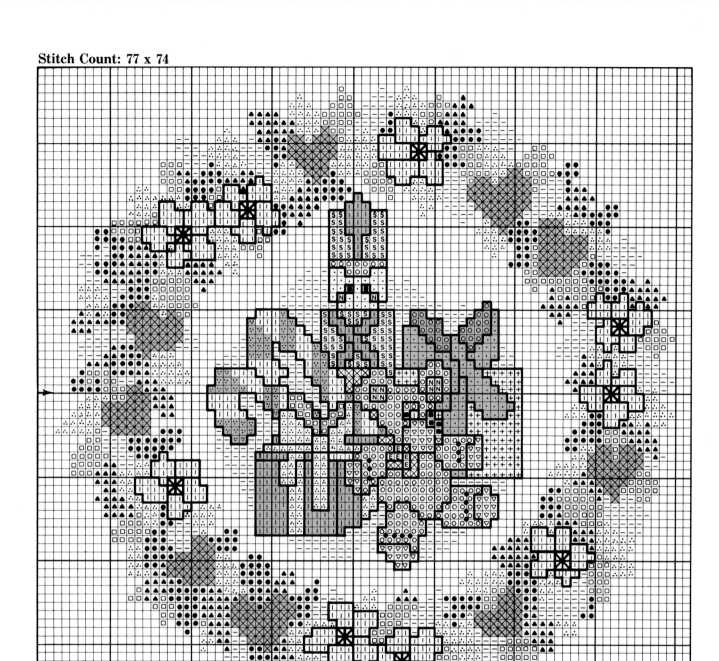

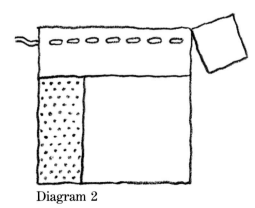

Diagram 2

6. Repeat Step 5 to add the border to the bottom and right edges of the Hardanger.

7. Repeat Steps 4 through 6 to attach the green border (Diagram 3).

8. With right sides of the pillow front and back together, stitch around the edge, leaving a 6″ opening in the bottom edge. Clip the corners and turn right side out. Place the pillow form inside and slipstitch the opening closed.

Diagram 3

Christmas Wishes Ornaments

Let your kids try cross-stitching these simple and fun-to-make ornaments. The thoughtful Christmas sayings were adapted to cross-stitch by Jo Buehler from her collection of sayings and verses.

SAMPLES

Stitched on white or cream Aida 18, the finished design size is 1½″ x 2″. The fabric was cut 7″ x 7″. Finished design sizes using other fabrics are Aida 11—2½″ x 3¼″; Aida 14—2″ x 2⅝″; Hardanger 22—1¼″ x 1⅝″.

Stitch Count: 29 x 36

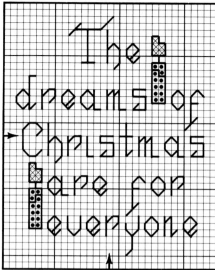

DREAMS OF CHRISTMAS

SUSAN BATES		DMC (used for sample)
		Step One: Cross-stitch (two strands)
306	☒	725 Topaz
216	●	367 Pistachio Green-dk.
		Step Two: Backstitch (one strand)
44		816 Garnet (lettering)
216		367 Pistachio green-dk. (candles)

Stitch Count: 28 x 36

LOVE OF CHRISTMAS

SUSAN BATES		DMC (used for sample)
		Step One: Cross-stitch (two strands)
44	■	816 Garnet (Red Heart Bead optional)
		Step Two: Backstitch (one strand)
879		890 Pistachio Green-ultra dk.

Stitch Count: 29 x 34

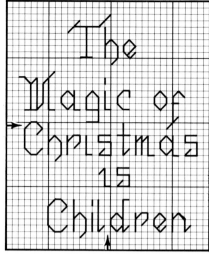

MAGIC OF CHRISTMAS

SUSAN BATES	DMC (used for sample)
	Step One: Backstitch (one strand)
44	816 Garnet

Stitch Count: 30 x 34

PRAYER OF CHRISTMAS

SUSAN BATES		DMC (used for sample)
		Step One: Cross-stitch (one strand)
	▲	Gold Metallic
		Step Two: Backstitch (one strand)
44		814 Garnet-dk.

Stitch Count: 28 x 38

HOPE OF CHRISTMAS

SUSAN BATES		DMC (used for sample)
		Step One: Backstitch (one strand)
879		890 Pistachio green-ultra dk.

Styrofoam Ornaments

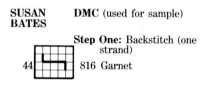

MATERIALS (for one ornament)
Completed cross-stitch on white or cream Aida 18; see sample information
Pencil
Small paring knife
Small piece of print fabric for back
One Styrofoam ball with a 3″ diameter
Pins
White glue
Assorted laces, trims, ribbons, buttons

DIRECTIONS
1. Draw a line around the center of the ball to divide it into two equal halves, or draw two parallel lines 1″ apart around the center of the ball.

2. Score the lines, using a paring knife.

3. From the print fabric, cut at least a 6½″ square to cover the back of the ball. Pin the fabric to the ball,

continued

making sure the fabric extends beyond the score line.

4. Using a paring knife, poke the fabric into the Styrofoam on the score line. Take small tucks as needed to mold the fabric over the round surface. Keep the score line as narrow and inconspicuous as possible. Trim any excess fabric.

5. Repeat Step 4; center design on the front half of the ball.

6. For an ornament with three sections, cut a strip 2″ x 11″, and repeat Step 4.

7. Glue lace, trim, or ribbon over the score line or lines and add ribbon bows as desired.

Stuffed Ornaments

MATERIALS (for one ornament)
Completed cross-stitch on white or cream Aida 18; see sample information
Tracing paper for pattern
Small piece of print fabric for back
Assorted laces, trims, ribbons
Stuffing

DIRECTIONS

1. Make a pattern for a 3½″ circle (see Appendix).

2. From the Aida, cut one circle with your design centered.

3. Cut one circle from the print fabric.

4. Baste the trim or lace to the right side of Aida, matching the raw edges.

5. Stitch the right sides of the Aida and print fabric together, leaving a 2″ opening. Turn right side out and stuff. Slipstitch the opening closed.

6. Attach a ribbon loop and bows as desired.

Kissing Ball

Attach a sprig of mistletoe to this pastel kissing ball and wait for your sweetheart to arrive.

SAMPLE

Stitched on white Aida 14, the finished design size is 4⅝″ x 4¾″. The fabric was cut 14″ x 14″. Finished design sizes in other fabrics are Aida 11—5⅞″ x 6⅛″; Aida 18—3⅝″ x 3¾″; Hardanger 22—3″ x 3″.

SUSAN BATES		DMC (used for sample)
		Step One: Cross-stitch (two strands)
386	·	746 Off-White
300	+	745 Yellow-lt. pale
297	U	743 Yellow-med.
304	E	741 Tangerine-med.
10	·	352 Coral-lt.
11	X	350 Coral-med.
50	o	605 Cranberry-vy. lt.
76	●	603 Cranberry
77	–	602 Cranberry-med.
108	△	211 Lavender-lt.
104	▲	210 Lavender-med.
130	X	799 Delft-med.
150	∴	823 Navy Blue-dk.
206	□	955 Nile Green-lt.
203	■	954 Nile Green
205	I	911 Emerald Green-med.
229	o	909 Emerald Green-vy. dk.
		Step Two: Backstitch (one strand)
150		823 Navy Blue-dk.

MATERIALS

Completed cross-stitch on white Aida 14; see sample information
⅜ yard of 45″-wide lavender print fabric; matching thread
2½ yards of ¼″-wide pink satin ribbon
1½ yards of ¹⁄₁₆″-wide purple satin ribbon
One Styrofoam ball with an 8″ diameter
Tacky glue
Felt-tip marker
Small paring knife
Ornament hook

DIRECTIONS

1. Mark a 2½″-wide band around the center of the ball. Score both edges.

2. From the lavender print fabric, cut one 12″ square. Center the piece over the back half of the ball and tuck it into the nearest score line. Trim any excess.

3. Repeat Step 2 with the Aida over the front half of the ball, centering the design.

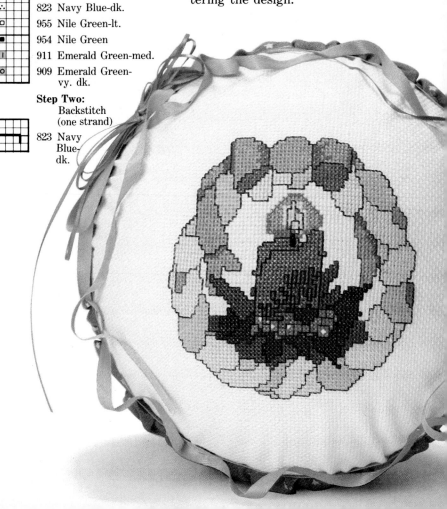

Stitch Count: 65 x 67

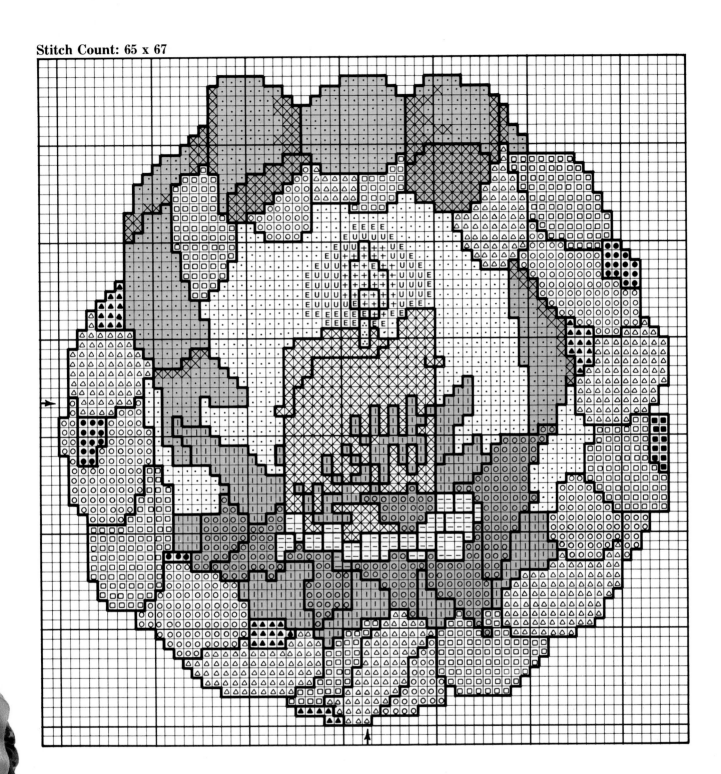

4. Also from the lavender print fabric, cut one 3½″ x 45″ piece. Gather both edges by hand or machine until the fabric equals 27″. Wrap it around the center band and tuck it into both score lines, distributing the fullness evenly.

5. Cut one 26″ length of pink ribbon. Glue the ribbon over the front seam using the glue sparingly. Cut one 30″ length and tie it into a 5″-wide bow; glue it to the upper left of the design. Drape the remaining pink ribbon around the edge of the Aida, spot-gluing as needed.

6. Cut one 10″ length of purple ribbon. Fold the remaining ribbon into 3″-wide loops and tie with a 10″ length; glue this over the pink bow.

7. Push the ornament hook through the fabric in the center of the top of the ball.

Christmas Bells

Ring in the holiday season with these festive Christmas bells. Using perforated paper allows you to cut and paste your stitching and create a three-dimensional design.

SAMPLE
Stitched on perforated paper 15, the finished design size for one motif is 2¾" x 1⅝". The bell pattern was traced onto perforated paper six times, and the placement of the stitching was marked on each. The finished design sizes using other fabrics are Aida 11—3½" x 2⅛"; Aida 18—2⅛" x 1¼"; Hardanger 22—1¾" x 1".

SUSAN BATES		DMC (used for sample)

Step One: Cross-stitch (three strands)

239	-	702 Kelly Green
923	X	699 Christmas Green
47	o	321 Christmas Red
371	■	433 Brown-med.

MATERIALS
Completed cross-stitch on perforated paper for six bell pieces; see sample information
Tracing paper for pattern
Two manila folders
Tacky glue
4 yards of ⅛"-wide fine cream trim
Red silk ribbon
Green silk ribbon

DIRECTIONS
1. From stitched perforated paper, cut six bell pieces.

2. Finishing option: On individual cross-stitched pieces, sew a running stitch with red ribbon ½" above the design (see photo). Sew another running stitch with the green silk ribbon ½" above the red ribbon. The running stitch may be repeated on the top portion of the bell if desired.

Stitch Count: 39 x 23

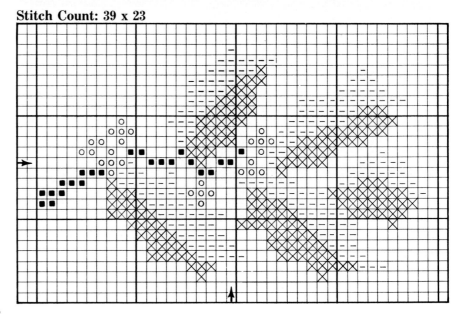

3. Transfer the pattern for the bell brace. Cut 6 braces from manila folders.

4. Glue the adjacent sides of all the braces together to make "spokes" (Diagram). Allow them to dry completely before proceeding.

Diagram

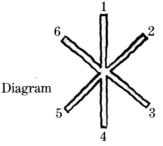

5. Glue the top halves of the perforated paper pieces 1, 3 and 5 to the braces, matching the edges of the paper with the edges of the braces. Hold each piece in place a short time to allow the glue to set, then allow it to dry. Glue the lower halves to the braces and allow them to dry completely before continuing.

6. Repeat Step 5 with pieces 2, 4, and 6.

7. Roll the scalloped edges of the perforated paper pieces, one at a time, around a pencil and hold them until a desired curve is achieved (see photo).

8. Cut three 15″ lengths of trim. Glue the trim over the seams, beginning above one scalloped edge and continuing to the opposite edge. Cut one 7″ length of trim and set aside. Use the remaining trim to glue around the scalloped edge. Make a loop for hanging the bell with the 7″ length, and glue it to the top of bell.

9. Tie bows with the red and green ribbons, and glue them to the top of the bell.

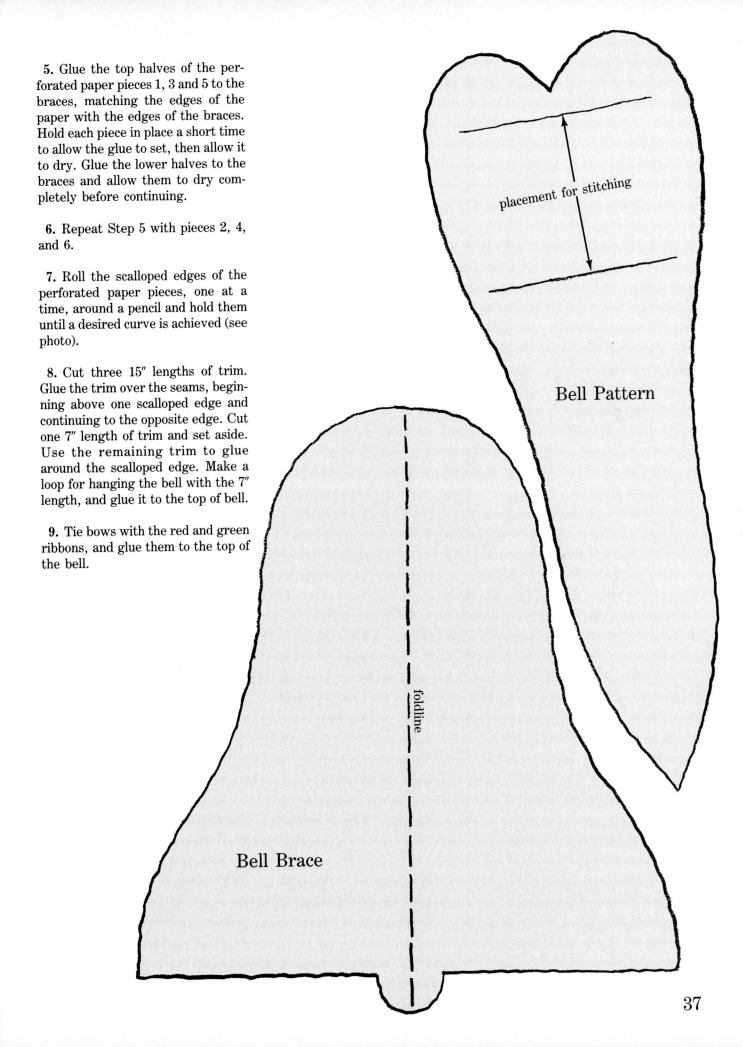

placement for stitching

Bell Pattern

Bell Brace

foldline

Stitch Count: 80 x 80

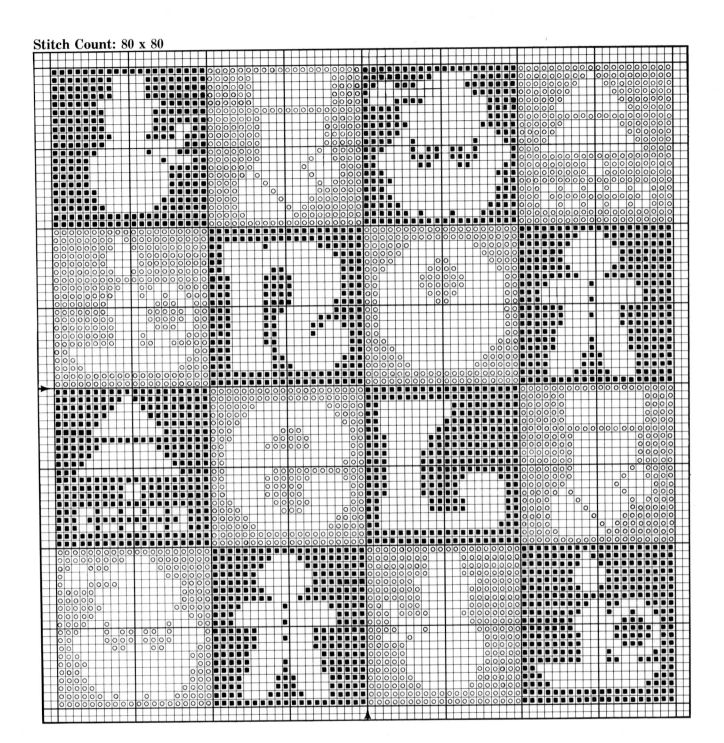

Noel Advent Calendar

Children will delight in counting down the days till Christmas with this cross-stitch Advent calendar. A piece of candy or a tiny ornament represents each day of the season.

SAMPLE

Stitched on Fiddlers Lite 14, the finished design size is 5¾″ x 5¾″. The fabric was cut 14″ x 20″. The design was stitched 4″ from the top edge and 4″ from the left edge of the fabric. Finished design sizes in other fabrics are Aida 11—7¼″ x 7¼″; Aida 14—5¾″ x 5¾″; Aida 18—4½″ x 4½″; Hardanger 22—3⅝″ x 3⅝″.

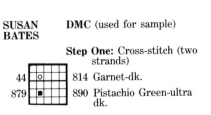

SUSAN BATES		DMC (used for sample)
		Step One: Cross-stitch (two strands)
44	o	814 Garnet-dk.
879	■	890 Pistachio Green-ultra dk.

continued

MATERIALS

Completed cross-stitch on Fiddlers
  Lite; see sample information
¾ yard of 45″-wide dark green
  print fabric; matching thread
Dressmaker's pen
1½ yards of green satin cording
  and burgundy satin cording
4½ yards of ¹⁄₁₆″-wide burgundy
  and/or green satin ribbon
Two 14″ stretcher bars
Two 20″ stretcher bars
One picture hanger
Staple gun
24 pieces of wrapped candy or 24
  small ornaments

DIRECTIONS

1. From Fiddlers Lite fabric, cut one 10″ x 16½″ piece with the design 2¼″ from the top (10″) edge and 2¼″ from the side (16½″) edge.

2. From the dark green fabric, cut two 6″ x 30″ pieces and two 6″ x 24″ pieces for the border.

3. Mark the centers of all the edges of the stitched piece and the center of one long edge of each green piece. Match the centers of one short border strip and the top of the cross-stitch piece. Place the right sides together and stitch to within ¼″ of the corners of the cross-stitch piece. Add the remaining three strips in the same manner.

4. To miter the corners, fold the right sides of two adjacent strips together and stitch at a 45-degree angle (Diagram). Trim the corners and press. Repeat for each corner.

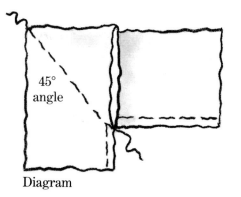

Diagram

45°
angle

5. With a dressmaker's pen, mark the placement for the satin cord. Mark rows 1½″, 3½″, and 5½″ below the design. Also mark eight 1″-wide units for each row.

6. Cut three 18″ lengths of satin cord from both colors. Separately knot one end of each color. Then handle both lengths as one and knot the cord 2½″ from the ends and at eight additional 1″ intervals. Repeat with the remaining cord.

7. Attach the knotted cord lengths to the cross-stitch piece by tacking the knots at the marks.

8. Assemble the stretcher bars, making sure the corners are square. Place the wall hanging wrong side up on a clean, flat surface. Center the stretcher bars over the fabric. Fold the center of one long side to the back of the stretcher bars and staple. Repeat with the center of the opposite long side, then the center of the short sides. Staple all the way around, alternating between sides until complete. Staple the corners, with as few folds as possible. Attach the picture hanger.

9. Cut the ribbon into 6″ lengths and tie candy to the calendar.

Lettuce Leaf Ornaments

Give these cross-stitch ornaments a "lettuce leaf" ruffle. Simply gather the inner circle, around the stuffing, to create this dainty effect.

SAMPLE

Stitched on white Linda 27 over two threads, the finished design sizes are—for the basket—1¼″ x 1⅜″; for the heart—1¼″ x 1¼″; for the flower—1¼″ x 1¼″; for the star—1⅜″ x 1⅜″.

Basket

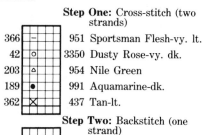

SUSAN BATES	DMC (used for sample)
	Step One: Cross-stitch (two strands)
366	951 Sportsman Flesh-vy. lt.
42	3350 Dusty Rose-vy. dk.
203	954 Nile Green
189	991 Aquamarine-dk.
362	437 Tan-lt.
	Step Two: Backstitch (one strand)
401	844 Beaver Grey-ultra dk.

Heart

SUSAN BATES	DMC (used for sample)
	Step One: Cross-stitch (two strands)
871	3041 Antique Violet-med.
215	369 Pistachio Green-vy. lt.
189	991 Aquamarine-dk.
885	739 Tan-ultra vy. lt.
362	437 Tan-lt.
	Step Two: Backstitch (one strand)
401	844 Beaver Grey-ultra dk.

Flower

SUSAN BATES	DMC (used for sample)
	Step One: Cross-stitch (two strands)
366	951 Sportsman Flesh-vy. lt.
8	761 Salmon-lt.
104	210 Lavender-med.
189	991 Aquamarine-dk.
	Step Two: Backstitch (one strand)
401	844 Beaver Grey-ultra dk.

Star

SUSAN BATES	DMC (used for sample)
	Step One: Cross-stitch (two strands)
366	951 Sportsman Flesh-vy. lt.
189	991 Aquamarine-dk.
42	3350 Dusty Rose-vy. dk.
362	437 Tan-lt.
203	954 Nile Green
	Step Two: Backstitch (one strand)
401	844 Beaver Grey-ultra dark

Stitch Count: 17 x 19

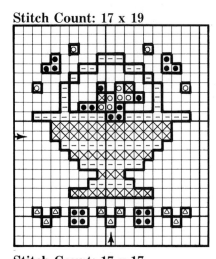

MATERIALS

Completed cross-stitch on white Linda; see sample information
Tracing paper for pattern
Small piece of colored fabric; matching thread
1¼ yards of ¹⁄₁₆″ or ⅛″-wide contrasting satin ribbon
White thread
Stuffing
Dressmaker's pen

Stitch Count: 17 x 17

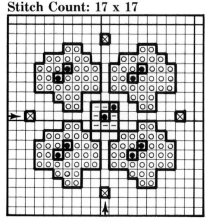

DIRECTIONS

1. Make the pattern for a 6″ circle (see Appendix).

2. From Linda, cut one circle with the design centered. Fold the edges ¼″ either to the right or the wrong side of fabric twice and slipstitch the hem by hand.

3. From the colored fabric, cut one circle. Fold the edges under ¼″ to the wrong side twice and hem by hand or machine.

4. On the right side of the Linda, mark another circle 1″ from the edge with a dressmaker's pen.

Stitch Count: 17 x 17

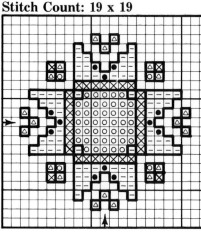

5. Place the Linda over the colored fabric. With white thread on the spool and colored thread on the bobbin, stitch on the pen line. Leave a 2″ opening.

6. Stuff the ornament and stitch the opening closed.

7. Sew a running stitch on the Linda ¼″ from the seam. Gather slightly and secure the thread.

8. Cut one 4″ length and one 15″ length of ribbon. Make a loop for hanging with the 4″ length and tack it to the back of the ornament. Wrap the remaining ribbon into 3″ wide loops and tie with the 15″ length. Tack to the ornament.

Stitch Count: 19 x 19

41

The children were nestled all snug in their beds...

While the children are nestled all snug in their beds, gather your needles and thread and create holiday memories in cross-stitch. Stitch a scene with the children at play in the snow or all dressed for the Sunday school Christmas pageant. Commemorate baby's first Christmas with a pillow of seasonal images or a colorful satin ribbon sampler of toys and holiday sweets. Make a special stocking with a tiny toy soldier and all kinds of adorable ornaments. A heavenly angel music box plays a favorite carol. There are even visions of sugarplums to stitch for the tree.

 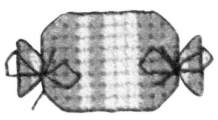 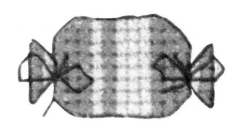

The Children Were Nestled

Visions of pink sugar plums playfully dance across this cross-stitch design while the angelic-looking child lies sleeping. The unusual color combination adds to the dreamlike quality of the design.

SAMPLE

Stitched on white Linda 27 over two threads, the finished design size is 10½" x 8⅛". The fabric was cut 17" x 14". Finished design sizes for other fabrics are Aida 11—12⅞" x 9⅞"; Aida 14—10⅛" x 7¾"; Aida 18—7⅞" x 6"; Hardanger 22—6⅜" x 5".

SUSAN BATES			DMC (used for sample)

Step One: Cross-stitch (two strands)

SUSAN BATES			DMC
1			White
293			727 Topaz-vy. lt.
306			725 Topaz
366			951 Sportsman Flesh-vy. lt.
4146			950 Sportsman Flesh-lt.
893			224 Shell Pink-lt.
49			3689 Mauve-lt.
66			3688 Mauve-med.
44			816 Garnet
44			814 Garnet-dk.
108			211 Lavender-lt.
159			827 Blue-vy. lt.
120			794 Cornflower Blue-lt.
940			792 Cornflower Blue-dk.
921			931 Antique Blue-med.
185			964 Seagreen-lt.
186			959 Seagreen-med.
188			943 Aquamarine-med.
189			991 Aquamarine-dk.
942			738 Tan-vy. lt.
363			436 Tan
309			435 Brown-vy. lt.
397			762 Pearl Grey-vy. lt.
8581			646 Beaver Grey-dk.

Step Two: Backstitch (one strand)

		DMC
940		792 Cornflower Blue-dk. (around letter *T*)
401		844 Beaver Grey-ultra dk. (all else)

Step Three: French Knots (one strand)

		DMC
44		816 Garnet
401		844 Beaver Grey-ultra dk.

Treasure Box

Keep quite safe what you like best—family photographs and sentimental mementos—in this cross-stitched treasure chest.

SAMPLE

Stitched on cream Hardanger 22 over two threads, the finished design size is 6½" x 4⅜". The fabric was cut 11" x 9". Finished design sizes for other fabrics are Aida 11—6½" x 4⅜"; Aida 14—5⅛" x 3⅜"; Aida 18—4" x 2⅝"; Hardanger 22—3¼" x 2⅛".

SUSAN BATES		DMC (used for sample)

Step One: Cross-stitch (three strands)

88	–	718 Plum
105	∴	209 Lavender-dk.
145	○	334 Baby Blue-med.
209	▲	913 Nile Green-med.
209	✕	913 Nile Green-med. (one strand)
357	■	801 Coffee Brown-dk.

Step Two: Backstitch (one strand)

| 357 | | 801 Coffee Brown-dk. (lettering) |
| 357 | | 801 Coffee Brown-dk. (two strands, rocking horses) |

Step Three: French Knots (one strand)

| 357 | • | 801 Coffee Brown-dk. |

MATERIALS

Completed cross-stitch on cream Hardanger; see sample information
Mat board
⅝ yard of 45"-wide muslin; matching thread
½ yard of 45"-wide polyester fleece
4" x 8" piece of flannel
1 yard of ⅜"-wide magenta grosgrain ribbon; matching thread
1⅝ yards of ¾"-wide cream cotton lace
⅛"-wide satin ribbons: 1¾ yards of light blue; 1⅜ yards of lavender; 1⅜ yards of light green

Top to bottom: Lion and Lamb, Treasure Box.

46

Stitch Count: 71 x 48

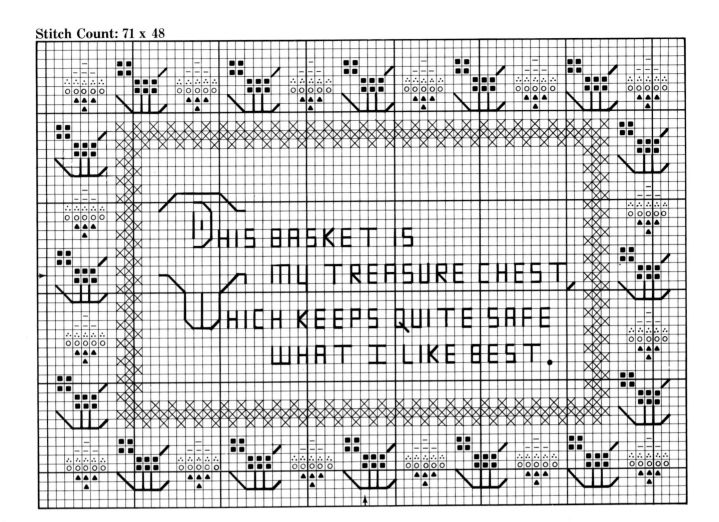

Four lavender ⅜″-wide heart buttons
Four aqua ⅜″-wide heart buttons
Two blue ⅜″-wide heart buttons
Strapping tape
X-Acto knife and straightedge
Dressmaker's pen

DIRECTIONS
All seam allowances are ¼″.

1. Cut the following pieces from the mat board: two 7¾″ x 5¾″ pieces for the lid and bottom; two 7¾″ x 3¼″ pieces for the sides; and two 5¾″ x 3¼″ pieces for the ends.

2. From Hardanger, cut one 8½″ x 6½″ piece with design centered.

3. Cut the following pieces from muslin: one 19½″ x 8½″ piece for the lining; four 6½″ x 4″ pieces for the ends; one 6½″ x 8½″ piece for the outside bottom; two 8½″ x 4″ pieces for the sides.

4. From the fleece, cut two 8½″ x 19½″ pieces and four 6½″ x 4″ pieces.

5. With right sides together, stitch the two side pieces to the bottom piece along the 8½″ edges.

6. With right sides together, stitch the 8½″ edge of one of the side pieces to the top edge of the Hardanger.

7. Pin corresponding fleece pieces to the wrong sides of outside unit and lining.

8. With right sides of the outside unit and lining together, stitch both long edges and the 8½″ edge of Hardanger. Trim fleece and clip corners. Turn right side out.

9. Insert one 7¾″ x 5¾″ piece of mat board behind the Hardanger and between the layers of fleece. Stitch by hand or by machine (using

a zipper-foot attachment) 6″ from the front edge through all the layers of fabric. This will hold the mat board in place.

10. Insert one 7¾″ x 3¼″ piece of mat board, the remaining 7¾″ x 5¾″ piece, and the second 7¾″ x 3¼″ piece between the layers of fleece. Slipstitch the opening closed. This mat board will support the back and bottom of the box.

11. Pin the remaining pieces of fleece to the wrong side of the end muslin pieces.

12. To make the ends of the box, place the right sides of two end muslin pieces together and stitch both the short edges and one long edge. Trim the fleece. Clip the corners and turn. Insert the mat board and slipstitch the opening closed. Repeat for the other end.

continued   **47**

13. To construct the box, fold the outside unit in place. Match the ends to the box front, back, and bottom. Slipstitch the pieces securely in place (Diagram 1).

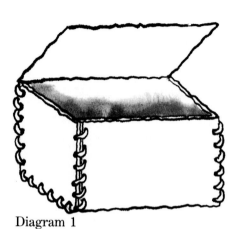

Diagram 1

14. Beginning in the corner, pin the grosgrain ribbon around the Hardanger with the outside edge of the ribbon ¼″ from the edge of the box (see photo). Slipstitch the ribbon to the Hardanger.

15. Cut the flat lace into two equal lengths. Slipstitch the straight edge of the lace around the top edge of the box. Repeat for the bottom edge of the box.

16. From the blue ribbon, cut two 3″ lengths. Thread the ends of one ribbon through two lavender buttons (Diagram 2). Fold the ribbon into a loop, and tack the loop to the center top edge of the front of the box (Diagram 3).

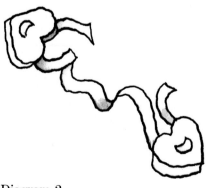

Diagram 2

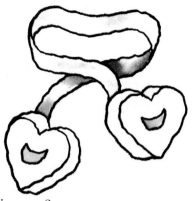

Diagram 3

17. Thread two aqua buttons onto the second ribbon. Tack the ends of the ribbon together and twist the ribbon into a figure eight (Diagram 4). Position the figure eight on the lid of the box so the button fits snugly in the bottom loop on the front of the box. Tack the figure eight to the center edge of the lid on the grosgrain ribbon.

Diagram 4

18. Tie a small bow with another blue ribbon. Tack the bow below the top button on the box lid (see photo).

19. Cut four 12″ lengths of ⅛″-wide ribbon from each color. Divide the ribbons into four groups of three colors. Tack the ends of two groups to the inside front corners of the box and the ends of the other two groups to the inside corners of the lid.

20. Thread the remaining buttons onto ribbon lengths and knot the ribbon ends.

The Lion and Lamb

The biblical theme of the peaceable kingdom, so popular with early American painters, continues to inspire designers today (see photo, page 46).

SAMPLE

Stitched on cream Hardanger 22 over two threads, the finished design size is 8⅜″ x 10⅞″. The fabric was cut 15″ x 16″. Finished design sizes for other fabrics are Aida 11—8⅜″ x 10⅞″; Aida 14—6⅝″ x 8⅝″; Aida 18—5⅛″ x 6⅝″; Hardanger 22—4⅛″ x 5½″.

SUSAN BATES		DMC (used for sample)
		Step One: Cross-stitch (three strands)
1		White
293		727 Topaz-vy. lt.
306		725 Topaz
49		3689 Mauve-lt.
69		3687 Mauve
70		3685 Mauve-dk.
43		815 Garnet-med.
43		815 Garnet-med. (bead sewn over cross-stitch)
978		322 Navy Blue-vy. lt.
215		368 Pistachio Green-lt.
242		989 Forest Green
216		320 Pistachio Green-med.
246		319 Pistachio Green-vy. dk.
307		783 Christmas Gold
309		781 Topaz-dk.
380		839 Beige Brown-dk.
397		762 Pearl Grey-vy. lt.
401		413 Pewter Grey-dk.
		Step Two: Backstitch (one strand)
70		3685 Mauve-dk. (on ribbon)
246		319 Pistachio Green-vy. dk. (star)
401		413 Pewter Grey-dk. (all else)
		Step Three: French Knots (one strand)
401		413 Pewter Grey-dk.
		Step Four: Long Stitch (one strand)
		Silver Metallic #22 smooth
		Step Five: Beadwork (sewn over cross-stitch)
		Red

Lollipops

Tuck cross-stitched lollipops among the gifts or hang them on the tree for extra treats.

SAMPLE

Stitched on white Linda 27 over two threads, the finished design size is 2¼" x 2½". The fabric was cut 6" x 6". Finished design sizes for other fabrics are Aida 11—2¾" x 3"; Aida 14—2⅛" x 2⅜"; Aida 18—1⅝" x 1⅞"; Hardanger 22 —1⅜" x 1½".

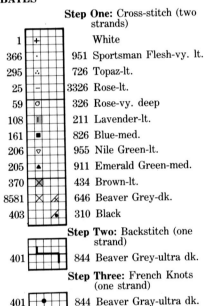

SUSAN BATES		DMC (used for sample)
		Step One: Cross-stitch (two strands)
1	+	White
366	·	951 Sportsman Flesh-vy. lt.
295	∴	726 Topaz-lt.
25	−	3326 Rose-lt.
59	o	326 Rose-vy. deep
108	l	211 Lavender-lt.
161	▪	826 Blue-med.
206	▽	955 Nile Green-lt.
205	▲	911 Emerald Green-med.
370	⊠	434 Brown-lt.
8581	⟋	646 Beaver Grey-dk.
403	⟋	310 Black
		Step Two: Backstitch (one strand)
401		844 Beaver Grey-ultra dk.
		Step Three: French Knots (one strand)
401	●	844 Beaver Gray-ultra dk.
403	○	310 Black

MATERIALS

Completed cross-stitch on white Linda; see sample information
Tracing paper for pattern
Small piece of cranberry print fabric; matching thread
1 yard of ⅛"-wide cranberry satin ribbon
One 12" length of ¼"-wide flat trim; matching thread
Stuffing
One sucker stick
White glue

Clockwise: Family Sampler, Lollipops, Heart Quilt and Pillow.

DIRECTIONS

1. Make a pattern for a 3¾"-wide circle (see Appendix).

2. For the lollipop front, cut one circle from the Linda with the design centered.

3. For the lollipop back, cut one circle from the cranberry print fabric. Also cut one 1" x 11" strip for the side.

4. Cut one 9" length of ribbon. Place glue on one end of the ribbon. Apply the glued end of the ribbon to the end of the sucker stick and spiral the ribbon around the stick to the opposite end; trim. Glue the second end of the ribbon to the stick. Set it aside and allow it to dry completely.

5. With the right sides together, stitch the side to the design piece beginning at the bottom of the design. Fold under the side ends ¼". Sew the cranberry print circle to the second long edge of the side, leaving a 2" opening in the center bottom. Turn and stuff firmly.

6. Tack the trim all the way around the side of the lollipop, beginning at the opening.

7. Apply glue to one end of the sucker stick and insert ½" of it into the stuffing through the opening. Slipstitch the opening closed, stitching very close to the stick.

8. Tie the remaining ribbon in a bow around the top of the stick.

Stitch Count: 30 x 33

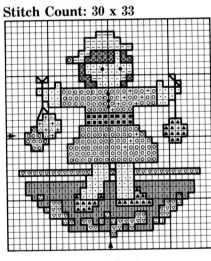

Stitch Count: 30 x 31

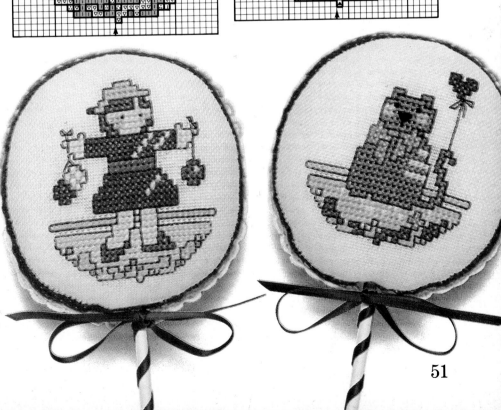

placement for stitching

Large Heart
Appliqué Pattern

Small Heart
Appliqué Pattern

fold line
cutting line

Heart Quilt and Pillow

Hearts cross-stitched with flowers embellish a matching quilt and pillow—a cozy nook for a friend (see photo, page 50).

SAMPLE

Stitched on white Aida 14, the finished design size of one heart is 3⅝" x 1¾". The fabric was cut 9" x 9". Finished design sizes for other fabrics are Aida 11—4⅝" x 2¼"; Aida 18—2⅞" x 1⅜"; Hardanger 22—2⅜" x 1⅛".

Stitch Count: 51 x 25

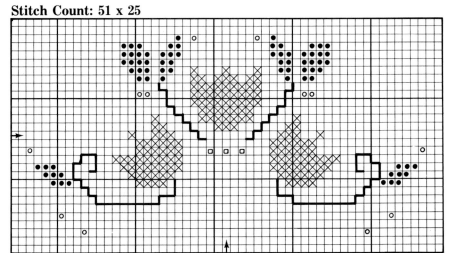

SUSAN BATES		DMC (used for sample)
		Step One: Cross-stitch (two strands)
303	o	742 Tangerine-lt.
47	X	321 Christmas Red
229	●	700 Christmas Green-bright
133	□	796 Royal Blue-dk.
		Step Two: Backstitch (two strands)
229		700 Christmas Green-bright

52

Heart Pillow

MATERIALS

Completed cross-stitch on white Aida; see sample information
Tracing paper for pattern
⅜ yard of 45″-wide blue pin-dot fabric; matching thread
⅜ yard of 45″-wide blue print fabric for the ruffle
Small piece of white print fabric for the borders
DMC floss #321
White thread
10″ x 10″ knife-edge pillow form

DIRECTIONS

1. Trace the pattern for the large heart, transferring all information.

2. From Aida, cut one heart with the design centered.

3. From the blue pin-dot fabric, cut one 10″ square and one 9″ square.

4. From the white print fabric, cut four 1″ x 10″ strips.

5. From the blue print fabric, cut four 2″ x 11″ pieces for the outside border. Also cut a 3½″-wide bias strip, piecing as needed, to equal 2½ yards.

6. Center the Aida heart on the 9″ blue pin-dot square. Fold the edges under ¼″ and slipstitch in place. Blanket-stitch around the heart with one strand of DMC 321.

7. Mark the centers of all four edges of the pin-dot square and the centers of one long edge of each outside border. Match the centers, right sides together, and stitch to within ½″ of the corners.

8. To miter the corners, fold the right sides of two adjacent strips together and stitch at a 45° angle (Diagram 1). Trim the seam allowances. Repeat for each corner.

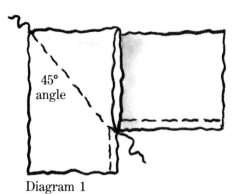

Diagram 1

9. Fold under the long edges of each white print strip ¼″ and press. Center the strips over the seam joining the center square and the border. Topstitch to the pillow top, overlapping at the corners.

10. To make the ruffle, fold the bias strip in half lengthwise and press. Divide it into fourths and mark on the raw edge. Stitch along the raw edge, gathering both layers. Match the marks on the ruffle to the corners of the pillow and gather to fit. Stitch the gathered edge to the pillow top, right sides together.

11. With right sides together, stitch the pillow back to the pillow top, leaving a 5″ opening in one edge. Turn and insert the pillow form. Slipstitch the opening closed.

Heart Quilt

MATERIALS

Completed cross-stitch on white Aida for three hearts; see sample information.
Tracing paper for patterns
3 yards of 45″-wide blue pin-dot fabric; matching thread
45″-wide print fabric: ½ yard of white, ⅜ yard of blue, ⅜ yard of green
Fusing material for the small hearts
Batting
DMC floss #321
White thread

DIRECTIONS

All seam allowances are ½″.

1. Transfer patterns for large and small heart; include all information.

2. From Aida, cut three large hearts with the designs centered.

3. From the blue pin-dot fabric, cut one 45″ square for the backing. Cut four 6″ x 45″ pieces for the border, two 4″ x 22″ pieces for the small heart panels and one 11″ x 20″ piece for the center panel. Also cut a 3″-wide bias strip, piecing as needed, to equal 5 yards.

4. From the white print fabric, cut two 2″ x 25″ pieces and two 2″ x 15″ pieces for the inside sashing. Cut four 2″ x 45″ pieces for the outside sashing. Also cut fourteen small hearts.

5. Cut twenty-four 4″ squares from the green print fabric and twenty-four squares from the blue print.

6. Cut fourteen small hearts from the fusing material.

7. Position the three Aida hearts on the center panel (Diagram 2). Fold the edges under ¼″ and slipstitch the hearts in place. Blanket-stitch around each one, using one strand of DMC 321.

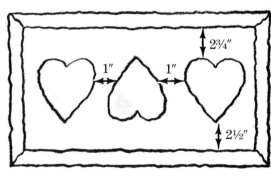

Diagram 2

continued

8. Mark the centers of all four edges of the center panel and the center of one edge of each of the four inside sashing strips. Match the center of one 15″ sashing strip and the end of the center panel. Stitch to within ½″ of the corners. Add the three remaining inside sashing strips to the sides of the panel.

9. To miter the corners, fold the right sides of two adjacent strips together and stitch at a 45° angle (Diagram 1). Trim the seam allowance. Repeat for each corner.

10. Alternating colors, stitch two blue and two green 4″ squares together. Sew this strip to one end of the center panel. Sew four more squares together and attach to the other end.

11. Center one small heart on both pin-dot background pieces with fusing material against the wrong side of the heart. Fuse according to the manufacturer's instructions. Place six more hearts on each background piece in the same manner.

12. With blue thread and medium-width stitches, satin-stitch by machine the edges of each small heart.

13. With right sides together, stitch a blue 4″ square to each end of one small heart panel. Stitch a green square to each end of the second panel.

14. With right sides together, stitch five green squares and four blue squares to one another, alternating colors. Repeat to make a second strip. Again alternating colors, stitch two more strips, each with five blue squares and four green squares.

15. Sew one of these strips of squares to each side of the two small heart panels, alternating the colors of the squares on the end. Sew these two sections to each side of the center panel. Alternate the colors of the end squares (Diagram 3).

16. With right sides together, stitch the outside sashing and the border to one another on the 45″ edge.

17. Mark centers of all edges of quilt and centers of remaining edges of outside sashing.

18. Matching centers, repeat the process described in Step 8 to attach the outside sashing and border. Repeat Step 9 to miter the corners.

19. Place the quilt backing on a flat surface with the wrong side up. Center the batting and quilt top right side up over the backing. Baste thoroughly.

20. Machine or hand-quilt around each Aida heart with matching thread. Also quilt both edges of the inside sashing, around the small heart panels, and both edges of the outside sashing.

21. Stitch the right sides of the bias strip and the quilt top together. Fold the bias double to the back of the quilt. Slipstitch it in place.

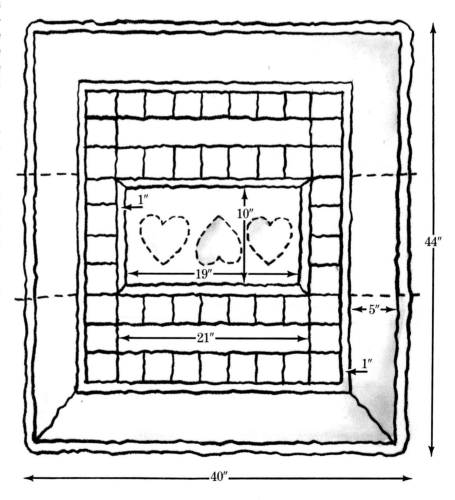

Diagram 3

54

Family Sampler

Welcome friends during the holidays—and all year long—with this colorful sampler and verse (see photos, pages 50 and 137).

SAMPLE

Stitched on cream Aida 14, the finished design size is 7⅞″ x 10⅞″. The fabric was cut 16″ x 19″. Finished design sizes for other fabrics are Aida 11—10″ x 13⅞″; Aida 18—6⅛″ x 8½″; Hardanger 22—5″ x 7″.

FINISHING OPTION

1¾ yard of ⅛″-wide red satin ribbon; white glue
Cut two 15″ lengths and two 12″ lengths of ribbon. Glue the 15″ lengths on each side of the design, ¾″ from the cross-stitch, and the 12″ lengths across the top and bottom of the design, ¾″ from the cross-stitch. Tie the remaining ribbon in a bow and tack in the lower right corner.

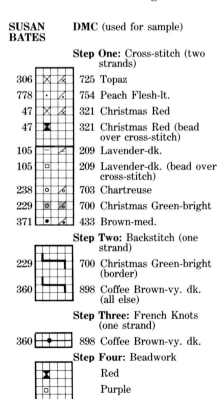

SUSAN BATES	DMC (used for sample)		
	Step One: Cross-stitch (two strands)		
306		725	Topaz
778		754	Peach Flesh-lt.
47		321	Christmas Red
47		321	Christmas Red (bead over cross-stitch)
105		209	Lavender-dk.
105		209	Lavender-dk. (bead over cross-stitch)
238		703	Chartreuse
229		700	Christmas Green-bright
371		433	Brown-med.
	Step Two: Backstitch (one strand)		
229		700	Christmas Green-bright (border)
360		898	Coffee Brown-vy. dk. (all else)
	Step Three: French Knots (one strand)		
360		898	Coffee Brown-vy. dk.
	Step Four: Beadwork		
			Red
			Purple

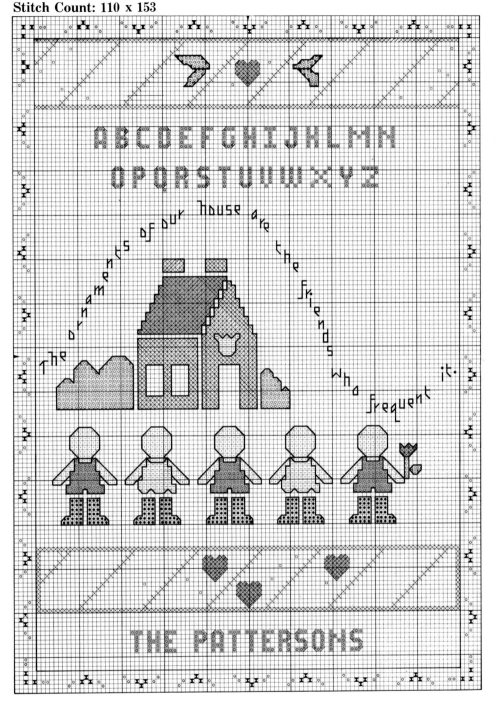

Afghan

Crochet this cozy afghan to ward off winter's chill and add a decorative touch to your family room. The cross-stitch is easy to add because the crocheted afghan stitches used for the panels make a perfect grid.

SAMPLE

Finished afghan measures approximately 35" x 63".

BUCILLA (used for sample)

Step One: Cross-stitch (one strand)

▢	203 Pale Rose
·	206 Medium Rose
▽	207 Dark Rose
─	26 Plum
▨	30 Violet
I	31 Dark Violet
○	25 Gray Purple
⊠	52 Dark Plum
⊠	214 Gray Blue
●	65 Teal Green
▲	225 Moss Green
⋮	57 Light Brown

Step Two: Backstitch (one strand)

206 Medium Rose (woman's dress)

25 Gray Purple (man's pants)

52 Dark Plum (man's shirt)

65 Teal Green (woman's apron, stems on side panels)

225 Moss Green (stems on center panel)

MATERIALS

7 to 9 skeins of Plymouth Scandi Fino White

Bucilla Persian Needlepoint and Crewel Wool in the following colors and quantities:

#203 Pale Rose-One 40 yd. skein

#206 Medium Rose-One 40 yd. skein

#207 Dark Rose-One 40 yd. skein

#26 Plum-Two 40 yd. skeins

#30 Violet-One 40 yd. skein

#31 Dark Violet-One 40 yd. skein

#25 Gray Purple-Two 40 yd. skeins

#52 Dark Plum-Two 40 yd. skeins

#214 Gray Blue-One 40 yd. skein

#65 Teal Green-One 40 yd. skein
#225 Moss Green-One 40 yd. skein
#57 Light Brown-One 40 yd. skein
Size F flexible afghan hook
Size F crochet hook
Large-eyed tapestry needle

DIRECTIONS
Gauge: 6 blocks per inch
1. Center panel (make 2)
With a size F afghan hook, chain 62.
Work afghan stitch for 144 rows.
When the piece totals 62 x 144
blocks, fasten off.

2. Side panel (make 4)
With a size F afghan hook, chain 20.
Work afghan stitch for 144 rows.
When the piece totals 20 x 144
blocks, fasten off.

3. Cross-stitch
Using a single strand of needlepoint
wool threaded on a large-eyed needle, complete the cross-stitch on
each piece according to the graphs.

4. Single crochet
Work 1 row of single crochet around
each panel, working 1 single crochet
in each block and 3 single crochet in
each corner. End with a slipstitch in
the first single crochet worked.

5. Lace panel (make 4)
Row 1: Chain 25. In the 4th chain
from the hook, work 2 double crochet, chain 2, then 2 double crochet.
*Skip 2 stitches. In next stitch,
work 1 double crochet, chain 1, 1
double crochet, skip 2 stitches. In
the next stitch, work 2 double crochet, chain 2, 2 double crochet. *Repeat between *s all the way across,
ending with a double crochet in last
stitch. Chain 2 and turn. **Row 2:**
Work 2 double crochet, chain 2, 2
double crochet in the first chain 2
space. *Double crochet, chain 2,
double crochet in the next chain 2
space, 2 double crochet, chain 2, 2
double crochet in the next chain 2
space. *Repeat across the row ending with 1 double crochet in the
turning chain. Chain 3, turn. Repeat
Row 2 until the piece is the same
length as the afghan-stitch panels.

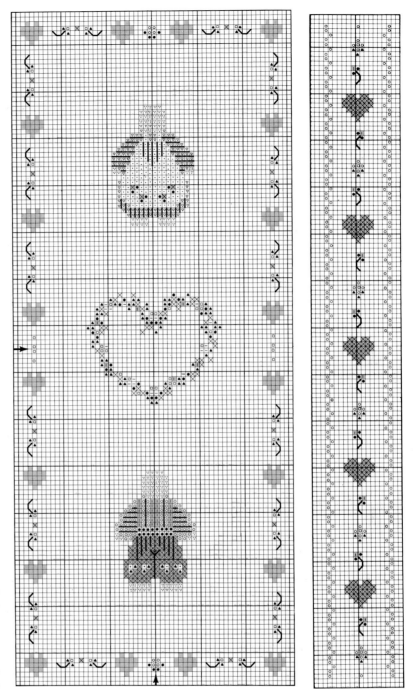

6. With matching yarn threaded on
a large-eyed needle, slipstitch the
lace panels between the afghan-
stitch panels.

7. Work Row 1 of the lace panel
and slipstitch it between the top and
bottom half of the afghan.

8. With the afghan right side up
and using #52 gray-purple needlepoint wool, single crochet 1 row
across the top and the bottom of the
afghan. Crochet a second row with

#26 gray-purple wool, and a third
row with #25 gray-purple wool.

9. Ruffle
Row 1: With the afghan right side
up, work * 2 double crochet, chain 2,
2 double crochet in a single crochet
at one corner of the afghan. Skip 2
single crochet. * Repeat between *s
around the entire afghan. **Row 2:**
Work 2 double crochet, chain 2, 2
double crochet in each chain 2 space
and each space between shells. Continue around the afghan. Fasten off.

Close-up of Winter Playground.

Within the design Winter Playground, Terrece Woodruff created three smaller designs. Here the left section of the design is stitched as a separate picture.

Winter Playground

Childhood memories of snowmen and sleigh rides in rural Idaho are reflected in a playful winter scene by Terrece Woodruff (see photo, page 59).

SAMPLE
Stitched on white Hardanger 22 over two threads, the finished design size is 21″ x 7⅝″. The fabric was cut 27″ x 14″. Finished design sizes for other fabrics are Aida 11—21″ x 7⅝″; Aida 14—16½″ x 6″; Aida 18—12¾″ x 4⅝″; Hardanger 22—10½″ x 3⅞″.

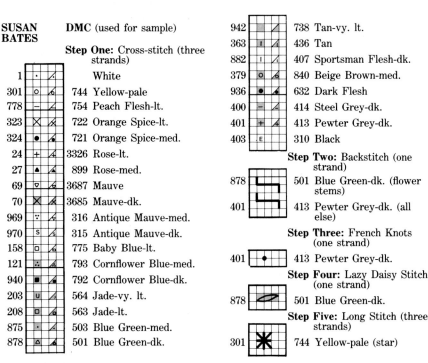

SUSAN BATES	DMC (used for sample)
	Step One: Cross-stitch (three strands)
1	White
301	744 Yellow-pale
778	754 Peach Flesh-lt.
323	722 Orange Spice-lt.
324	721 Orange Spice-med.
24	3326 Rose-lt.
27	899 Rose-med.
69	3687 Mauve
70	3685 Mauve-dk.
969	316 Antique Mauve-med.
970	315 Antique Mauve-dk.
158	775 Baby Blue-lt.
121	793 Cornflower Blue-med.
940	792 Cornflower Blue-dk.
203	564 Jade-vy. lt.
208	563 Jade-lt.
875	503 Blue Green-med.
878	501 Blue Green-dk.
942	738 Tan-vy. lt.
363	436 Tan
882	407 Sportsman Flesh-dk.
379	840 Beige Brown-med.
936	632 Dark Flesh
400	414 Steel Grey-dk.
401	413 Pewter Grey-dk.
403	310 Black
	Step Two: Backstitch (one strand)
878	501 Blue Green-dk. (flower stems)
401	413 Pewter Grey-dk. (all else)
	Step Three: French Knots (one strand)
401	413 Pewter Grey-dk.
	Step Four: Lazy Daisy Stitch (one strand)
878	501 Blue Green-dk.
	Step Five: Long Stitch (three strands)
301	744 Yellow-pale (star)

Christmas Is For Children

The innocence and spirit of the annual Christmas pageant are captured here in cross-stitch.

SAMPLE

Stitched on white Jobelan 28 over two threads, the finished design size is 7″ x 8⅜″. The fabric was cut 13″ x 15″. Finished design sizes for other fabrics are Aida 11—8⅞″ x 10⅝″; Aida 14—7″ x 8⅜″; Aida 18—5½″ x 6½″; Hardanger 22—4½″ x 5⅜″.

SUSAN BATES			DMC (used for sample)
			Step One: Cross-stitch (two strands)
387	I		712 Cream
300	o		745 Yellow-lt. pale
778	-		754 Peach Flesh-lt.
9	X		760 Salmon
66	△		3688 Mauve-med.
42	+		309 Rose-deep
104	+		210 Lavender-med.
105	●		209 Lavender-dk.
128			800 Delft-pale
130	o		809 Delft
121	X		793 Cornflower Blue-med.
210	□		562 Jade-med.
212	▼		561 Jade-vy. dk.
882	·		407 Sportsman Flesh-dk.
936	●		632 Dark Flesh
397	·		762 Pearl Grey-vy. lt.
398	s		415 Pearl Grey

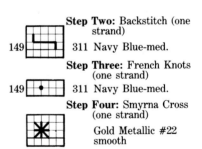

Step Two: Backstitch (one strand)

149   311 Navy Blue-med.

Step Three: French Knots (one strand)

149   311 Navy Blue-med.

Step Four: Smyrna Cross (one strand)

Gold Metallic #22 smooth

Lamb Pillow

The combination of buttons, tucks, delicate colors, and a charming cross-stitch design produces a delightful gift for a new mother.

SAMPLE

Stitched on aqua Aida 14, the finished design size is 6⅛" x 1⅞". The fabric was cut 12" x 10". Finished design sizes for other fabrics are Aida 11—7⅞" x 2⅜"; Aida 18—4¾" x 1½"; Hardanger 22—3⅞" x 1⅛".

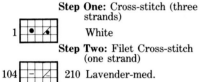

| SUSAN BATES | DMC (used for sample) |

Step One: Cross-stitch (three strands)

1   White

Step Two: Filet Cross-stitch (one strand)

104   210   Lavender-med.

MATERIALS

Completed cross-stitch on aqua Aida 14; see sample information
One 10" x 8¼" piece of unstitched aqua Aida 14; matching thread
⅜ yard of lavender fabric; matching thread
2½ yards of ⅛"-wide lavender satin ribbon
⅜ yard of ¹⁄₁₆"-wide lavender satin ribbon
⅜ yard of ⅛"-wide aqua satin ribbon

Clockwise: Goose Sampler, Angel Music Box, Lamb Pillow.

50 small lavender beads
Five ⅛"-wide lavender pearl shank buttons
Two ¼"-wide lavender shank buttons
Stuffing

DIRECTIONS

1. Weave the ¹⁄₁₆"-wide lavender ribbon over two threads, under two threads across the stitched aqua Aida fabric, ¾" below the bottom edge of the design. Tack the ends of the ribbon in place.

2. Using lavender thread, couch an aqua ribbon in place, one thread unit below the lavender ribbon.

3. To make the tucks, fold the Aida, wrong sides together, ½" below the aqua ribbon and 1" above the top edge of the design. Using matching thread, sew a seam by hand ¼" from the folds. Press the tucks toward the design.

4. Beginning 1¼" outside the design, sew the small beads over the seam line of the tucks, spacing the beads four thread units apart.

5. Center and stitch ⅛"-wide buttons ½" below the bottom edge of the design, spacing the buttons 1" apart. Stitch one ¼"-wide button on each end 1" from the other buttons.

6. From the stitched Aida, cut one 10" x 8¼" piece; center the design.

7. From the lavender fabric, cut one 10" x 16" piece for the lining. Also cut two 9½" x 7½" pieces for the pillow.

8. Stitch the right sides of two 9½" x 7½" lavender pieces together, leaving a 3" opening on one long side. Trim the corners and turn right side out. Stuff; slipstitch the opening closed.

9. With the right sides of two Aida pieces together, stitch a ½" seam in both 10" edges, leaving the short ends open to form a tube.

10. With the right sides of the remaining lavender piece together, stitch a ¼" seam in the 10" edges to form a tube.

11. With the right sides together, slip the lavender lining over the Aida. Stitch around one edge and turn. Fold in the seam allowance of the opposite side and slipstitch.

12. Cut the remaining lavender ribbon into eight equal lengths. Tack one length to the lining inside the pillow cover under each tuck. Tack another ribbon to the lining back opposite the tuck.

13. Slide the pillow inside the cover and tie the ribbons in bows to hold the pillow inside.

Stitch Count: 86 x 26

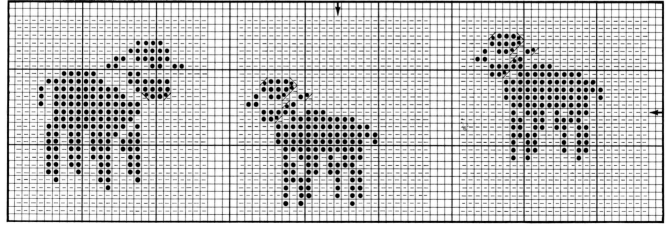

Angel Music Box

Find the musical works for your favorite carol, place them inside a cross-stitch pillow, and you will have your own unique music box. (Musical works are available at craft stores.)

SAMPLE

Stitched on cream Linda 27 over two threads, the finished design size is 4⅝" x 5¾". The fabric was cut 9" x 10". Finished design sizes for other fabrics are Aida 11—5¾" x 7"; Aida 14— 4½" x 5½"; Aida 18—3½" x 4¼"; Hardanger 22—2⅞" x 3½".

SUSAN BATES			DMC (used for sample)
			Step One: Cross-stitch (two strands)
386	–		746 Off-White
292	s		3078 Golden Yellow-vy. lt.
301	o		744 Yellow-pale
303	●		742 Tangerine-lt.
307	☒		977 Golden Brown-lt.
778	I		754 Peach Flesh-lt.
893	△		224 Shell Pink-lt.
893	∴		224 Shell Pink-lt. (bead over cross-stitch)
869	☒		3042 Antique Violet-lt.
158	□		747 Sky Blue-vy. lt.
213	·		369 Pistachio Green-vy. lt.
215	▲		368 Pistachio Green-lt.
876	■		502 Blue Green
387	o		822 Beige Grey-lt.
			Step Two: Backstitch (one strand)
897			221 Shell Pink-dk.
215			368 Pistachio Green-lt.
8581			3022 Brown Grey-med.
			Step Three: Beadwork
			Mauve (bead over cross-stitch)

MATERIALS

Completed cross-stitch on cream Linda; see sample information
¼ yard of unstitched cream Linda; matching thread
1½ yards of ⅜"-wide lavender satin ribbon; matching thread
¾ yard of small cording
Stuffing
2" x 4" music box

DIRECTIONS

1. For the front, cut the stitched Linda 7¼" x 6¼" with the design centered. Zigzag the edges.

2. For the back, cut the unstitched Linda 7¼" x 6¼". Zigzag the edges. Also cut 1½"-wide bias strips, piecing as needed, to equal 27". Cover 27" of cording.

3. Stitch the cording to the front of the stitched Linda.

4. In the center of unstitched piece, make a ¾" buttonhole for the windup key of the music box.

5. With right sides together, stitch the front to the back on the stitching line of the cording. Leave a 3" opening and turn.

6. Stuff the front and insert the music box, pushing the windup key through the buttonhole. Stuff the back until it is firm. Slipstitch the opening closed.

7. Cut one 30" and two 12" lengths of ribbon. Working with one end of the 30" length of ribbon, fold the ribbon into a 1½"-deep loop and a 1¼"-deep loop (see Diagram). Tack it securely through all layers of ribbon to the corner of the music box. Repeat at the second corner.

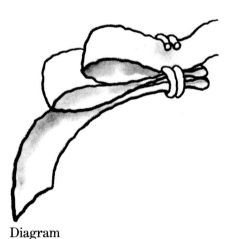

Diagram

8. With the remaining ribbons, tie two small bows. Tack a bow to each top corner of the music box (see photo).

Goose Sampler

In this adorable sampler, graphic design and subtle pastel shading are cleverly combined with traditional sampler elements such as the alphabet and geese.

SAMPLE
Stitched on white Jobelan 28 over two threads, the finished design size is 7¼" x 10". The fabric was cut 13" x 16". Finished design sizes for other fabrics are Aida 11—9⅛" x 12¾"; Aida 14—7¼" x 10"; Aida 18—5⅝" x 7¾"; Hardanger 22—4⅝" x 6⅜".

SUSAN BATES		DMC (used for sample)
		Step One: Cross-stitch (two strands)
1	∴	White
292	−	3078 Golden Yellow-vy. lt.
297	E	743 Yellow-med.
306	Z	725 Topaz
868	S	758 Terra Cotta-lt.
49	I	963 Dusty Rose-vy. lt.
74	□	3354 Dusty Rose-lt.
42	■	3350 Dusty Rose-vy. dk.
969	U	316 Antique Mauve-med.
871	N	3041 Antique Violet-med.
108	·	211 Lavender-lt.
104	+	210 Lavender-med.
110	▽	208 Lavender-vy. dk.
117	o	341 Blue Violet-lt.
158	·	828 Blue-ultra lt.
159	I	827 Blue-vy. lt.
128	⊠	800 Delft-pale
160	⊠	813 Blue-lt.
131	●	798 Delft-dk.
203	⋮	564 Jade-vy. lt.
185	⊙	964 Seagreen-lt.
187	⊟	992 Aquamarine
398	△	415 Pearl Grey
399	▲	318 Steel Grey-lt.
		Step Two: Backstitch (one strand)
149		311 Navy Blue-med.
		Step Three: French Knots (one strand)
149		311 Navy Blue-med.

Borrow the geese from the pastel sampler to decorate a detachable collar for your little girl.

Angel Pinafore

Rows of whimsical angels form a pastel Christmas tree on the bib of this little girl's pinafore. Cross-stitching can provide an original look to your children's clothing, and a pinafore is an ideal canvas for your work, since it can be worn for several seasons. On page 24 you can see the same funny little angels in a candle ring design.

SAMPLE

Stitched on white Linda 27 over two threads, the finished design size is 6⅝″ x 7⅝″. The fabric was cut 14″ x 14″. When using this design or portions of it for clothing, compare the finished design size of the desired motifs with the desired pattern piece. Finished design sizes for other fabrics are Aida 11—8⅛″ x 9⅜″; Aida 14—6⅜″ x 7⅜″; Aida 18—5″ x 5¾″; Hardanger 22—4″ x 4⅝″.

SUSAN BATES		DMC (used for sample)	

Step One: Cross-stitch (two strands)

1		White
386		746 Off-White
288		445 Lemon-lt.
778		754 Peach Flesh-lt.
24		776 Pink-med.
105		209 Lavender-dk.
167		519 Sky Blue
264		772 Pine Green-lt.
206		955 Nile Green-lt.
942		738 Tan-vy. lt.
914		3064 Sportsman Flesh-med.

Step Two: Backstitch (one strand)

380		839 Beige Brown-dk.

Step Three: French Knots (one strand)

380		839 Beige Brown-dk.

Top to bottom: Kissing Ball, Soft-Sculpture Dove, Angel Pinafore.

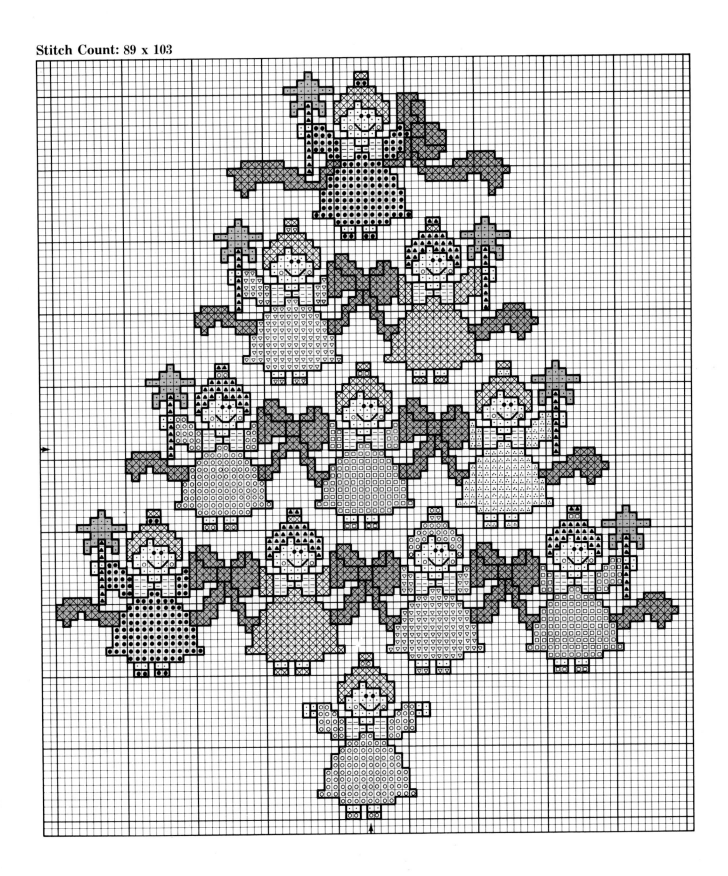

Satin Candy Canes

Red and white ribbon candy cane ornaments and sachets will brighten your tree and sweeten your room (with peppermint scent, of course), and they won't melt in helpful little hands.

SAMPLE

Stitched on white Hardanger 22 over two threads, the finished design size is 7/8" x 2⅛". The fabric was cut 7" x 7". See graph for "Shaun's First Christmas" (page 75).

MATERIALS

Completed design on white Hardanger 22: see sample information
Small amounts of white fabric and red fabric with white stripes; white thread
Satin ribbon: 1 yard of 1/16"-wide green, ½ yard of ⅛"-wide red, ½ yard of ⅛"-wide white
Large-eyed needle
Stuffing
Optional: Small amount of potpourri or peppermint oil

DIRECTIONS

1. From the Hardanger, cut one 4½" square with the design centered, for the ornament front.

2. From the white fabric, cut one 4½" square for the ornament back. Also cut one 2" x 16½" piece to back the shirring.

3. Cut 2"-wide bias strips from the red fabric with white stripes, piecing as needed to equal 1 yard for shirring.

Top to bottom: Shaun's First Christmas, Satin Candy Canes, Toy Soldier Stocking, Red Ribbon Hearts.

4. Stitch gathering threads on both long edges of the shirring strip and gather until it measures 16½".

5. With the right side out, pin the shirring strip to the shirring backing. Stitch both long edges through all the thicknesses.

6. Match the short ends of the shirred strip with right sides together and stitch to make one continuous piece. Divide this continuous piece into quarters and mark. Also mark the centers of the edges of the front and back pieces.

7. With the right sides together, match the marks on the shirred strips to the marks on the front of the ornament. Stitch, pivoting at corners. Trim the seam allowance.

8. Repeat Step 7 with the second long edge of the shirred strip and the back of the ornament, leaving a 2" opening on one side. Turn right side out.

9. Stuff firmly (potpourri or oil may be added if desired) and slipstitch the opening closed.

10. Using the green ribbon and a large-eyed needle, sew a running stitch around the front of the ornament. Begin in the upper right corner, leaving a 12" tail of ribbon.

11. Handle the white and red ribbons as one and tie them into a 3"-wide bow. Use the tails of the green ribbon and tie a bow around the center of the white and red bow.

Red Ribbon Hearts

Hearts of red ribbon say "Merry Christmas" in a special way on this easy-to-make pillow.

SAMPLE

Stitched on white Hardanger 22 over two threads, the finished design size is 3½" x 3¾". The fabric was cut 8" x 8". To stitch the hearts, see the heart on the graph for "Shaun's First Christmas" (page 75). Three hearts were stitched on two rows, but the third horizontal row has only two hearts. The hearts are spaced seven thread units apart. The rows are spaced six thread units apart.

MATERIALS

Completed design on white Hardanger 22; see sample information
One 6" square of white fabric for the back; matching thread
Small amount of red check fabric for the cording
¾ yard of small cording
½ yard of ⅛"-wide red satin ribbon
½ yard of ⅛"-wide white satin ribbon
Stuffing
Optional: Small amount potpourri

DIRECTIONS

1. From the Hardanger, cut one 6" square with the design centered for the front.

2. From the red check fabric, cut 1¼"-wide bias strips, piecing as needed, to equal 27". Cover the cording.

3. Stitch the cording to the right side of the design piece, matching the raw edges and using a ½" seam allowance. Clip the seam allowance of the cording at the corners.

4. With right sides together, stitch the white fabric piece to the Hardanger design on the stitching line of the cording. Leave a 3" opening and turn right side out.

5. Stuff firmly (potpourri may be added if desired), and slipstitch the opening closed.

6. Handle both ribbons as one and tie a 3 ¾"-wide bow. Tack the bow to the upper left corner of the front.

Shaun's First Christmas

Celebrate the magic of your baby's first Christmas with this sampler of Christmas images created by Terrece Woodruff for her own son (see photo, page 72).

SAMPLE

Stitched on white Hardanger 22 over two threads, the finished design size is 9⅛" x 10⅛". The fabric was cut 15" x 16".

MATERIALS

Satin ribbons are needed in the following amounts, widths, and colors:

2¼ yards of ⅛"-wide lavender
9¼ yards of ¹⁄₁₆"-wide blue
3 yards of ¹⁄₁₆"-wide red
1⅞ yards of ¹⁄₁₆"-wide green
1⅝ yards of ¹⁄₁₆"-wide lavender
1⅜ yards of ¹⁄₁₆"-wide mint
1¾ yards of ¹⁄₁₆"-wide grape
1 yard of ¹⁄₁₆"-wide light pink
¼ yard of ¹⁄₁₆"-wide white
¼ yard of ¹⁄₁₆"-wide yellow
Thread to match the ribbon colors

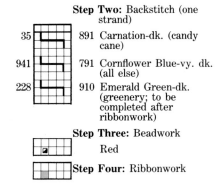

SUSAN BATES	DMC (used for sample)
	Step One: Cross-stitch (three strands)
1	White
293	727 Topaz-vy. lt. (one strand)
306	725 Topaz (one strand)
306	725 Topaz
307	783 Christmas Gold
49	963 Dusty Rose-vy. lt.
26	894 Carnation-vy. lt.
35	891 Carnation-dk.
105	209 Lavender-dk.
161	826 Blue-med.
940	792 Cornflower Blue-dk.
206	955 Nile Green-lt.
209	913 Nile Green-med.
228	910 Emerald Green-dk.
362	437 Tan-lt.
309	435 Brown-vy. lt.
371	433 Brown-med.

	Step Two: Backstitch (one strand)
35	891 Carnation-dk. (candy cane)
941	791 Cornflower Blue-vy. dk. (all else)
228	910 Emerald Green-dk. (greenery; to be completed after ribbonwork)
	Step Three: Beadwork
	Red
	Step Four: Ribbonwork

DIRECTIONS

All ribbons are ¹⁄₁₆" wide unless otherwise noted. Tack all the ribbon ends on the wrong side of the stitched piece. To complete the borders around the blocks, cut the lengths of ribbon as specified in the directions for each block. Lay one ribbon length in place on each side of the block. Thread the ribbon ends to the wrong side of the stitched piece, as indicated on the graph, and tack them together. Repeat with the ribbon lengths at the top and bottom of the block. Couch on the couching lines with matching thread (see graph).

1. Candle

Using a 6" length of lavender ribbon, vertically satin-stitch the top part of the candle. Using an 8" length of grape ribbon, vertically satin-stitch the bottom part of the candle. Using a 3" length of yellow ribbon, sew a lazy daisy stitch for the flame. For the border, use four 4" lengths of lavender ribbon. Complete backstitching of the greenery over the ribbonwork.

2. Heart

Using a 12" length of red ribbon, vertically satin-stitch the heart. Use four 4" lengths of blue ribbon for the inside border and four 4" lengths of mint ribbon for the outside border.

3. Doll

Using a 16" length of red ribbon, satin-stitch vertical rows on the bodice of the dress. Using a 16" length of light pink ribbon, stitch horizontal rows on the bodice, weaving them through the vertical ribbons. Using a 16" length of red ribbon, vertically satin-stitch the skirt. Couch on the couching lines with matching thread (see graph). Using a 10" length of red ribbon, horizontally satin-stitch the shoes. For the double border of the upper block around the doll, use six 4" lengths of blue ribbon for sides and top. Also use one 1½" length of blue ribbon for the bottom borders between the arm and the skirt of the doll. For the border of the lower block around the doll, use three 4" lengths and one 2" length of green ribbon.

4. Candy Cane

Using an 18" length of red ribbon, vertically satin-stitch the bands on the candy cane. Couch on the couching lines with matching thread (see graph).

5. Rocking Horse

Using a 14" length of red ribbon, satin-stitch vertical rows on the saddle. Using another 14" length of red ribbon, stitch horizontal rows on the saddle, weaving through the vertical ribbons. Using a 7" length of blue ribbon, satin-stitch two vertical rows for stirrups. For the inside border around the tail, use three 3" lengths and one 2½" length of light pink ribbon. Use six 4" lengths and two 2½" lengths of blue ribbon for the middle and outside borders. For the inside border on the block around the head, use four 4" lengths of green ribbon. Use four 4" lengths and four 2½" lengths of lavender ribbon for the middle and the outside borders. For the inside and middle border on the block around the tail, use eight 4" lengths of mint ribbon. Use four 4" lengths of grape ribbon for the outside border. For the inside border on the block around the stirrup, use three 2½" lengths of light pink ribbon. Use two 4" lengths and two 2½" lengths of green ribbon for the middle and the outside borders; cover the lower right bottom border as indicated on the graph.

Stitch Count: 101 x 111

6. Star

Using a 16″ length of blue ribbon, satin-stitch the horizontal and vertical rows of the star (see photo). Using a 16″ length of grape ribbon, satin-stitch the remaining rows. For the border, use four 4″ lengths of blue ribbon.

7. Soldier

Using two 2½″ lengths of white ribbon, sew an X across the front of the soldier. Using a 4½″ length of red ribbon, sew long stitches for the plume. Using a 3″ length of yellow ribbon, satin-stitch horizontal bands on the hat. Using a 22″ length of green ribbon, satin-stitch vertical and horizontal rows of greenery next to the soldier, threading the ribbon behind the cross-stitch as indicated on graph.

8. Name Block

Use one 4″ length and two 9″ lengths of grape ribbon.

9. Stars

For each small star on the background, sew a cross, using a 4″ length of blue ribbon. For the larger star, sew an X, using a 5″ length of lavender ribbon (see photo). Sew a cross over the lavender X, using a 5″ length of blue ribbon. Couch the center of all the stars with matching thread as indicated on the graph.

INSIDE BORDERS

Use four 16″ lengths and four 14″ lengths of blue ribbon.

OUTSIDE BORDERS

Use two 21″ lengths and two 19″ lengths of ⅛″-wide lavender ribbon for the inside border. Use two 21″ lengths and two 19″ lengths of blue ribbon for the outside border.

BOW

Using a 5″ length of lavender ribbon, tie a 1″-wide bow and tack it to the right side of the neck of the teddy bear.

Toy Soldier Stockings

Quick and easy to stitch, a toy soldier is the perfect motif for your favorite little boy's stocking (see photo, page 72). The hearts and the soldier are borrowed from the graph for "Shaun's First Christmas" (page 75) and are worked in ribbon and embroidery floss. (For a girl, just replace the soldier with an angel or a doll.)

SAMPLE

Stitched on white Linda 27 over two threads, the finished design size is 2½″ x 2½″. The fabric was cut 12″ x 12″. The stitching begins at the top of the soldier, 3½″ below the top edge of the fabric, and is centered horizontally. The soldier and hearts are spaced four thread units apart.

MATERIALS

Completed design on white Linda; see sample information
Tracing paper for pattern
8″ x 11″ piece of unstitched white Linda; matching thread
¼ yard of 45″-wide blue print fabric; matching thread
¾ yard of ⅛″-wide red satin ribbon
¾ yard of ⅛″-wide white satin ribbon
⅝ yard of ¹⁄₁₆″-wide red satin ribbon
¼ yard of polyester fleece
Large-eyed needle
Dressmaker's pen

DIRECTIONS

1. Trace the stocking pattern, transferring all the information.

2. From the stitched Linda, cut one stocking piece with the toe pointing left, for the stocking front. Position the design 2½″ below the top edge and center it horizontally. Zigzag the edges to keep them from raveling.

3. From the unstitched Linda, cut one stocking piece with the toe pointing right, for the back of the stocking. Zigzag the edges.

4. From the blue print fabric, cut two opposite stocking pieces for the lining, adding ¼″ to the top edges of the stocking (see pattern). Cut one 13″ x 1½″ strip for the shirred band. Also cut one 3½″ x 9″ bias strip for the shirred toe.

5. Cut two stocking pieces from the fleece.

6. Stitch two rows of gathering threads ⅛″ and ¼″ from both long edges of the strip for the shirred band. Gather the band 1¼″ from the top edge until it measures 5¾″.

7. Draw two lines across the top of the stocking front (Diagram 1). Cut along these lines to form Piece A and Piece B. With right sides together, match one edge of the shirred band to the top edge of Piece B and stitch. With right sides together, match the remaining edge of the shirred band to the bottom edge of Piece A and stitch.

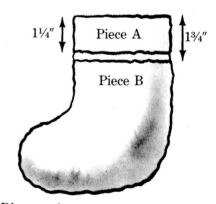

Diagram 1

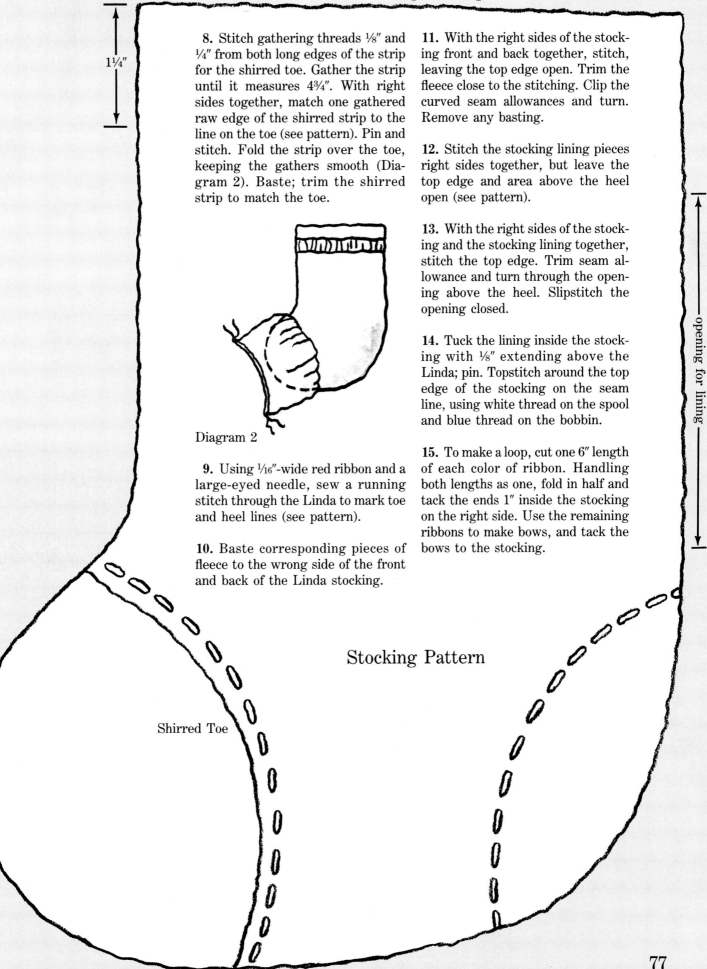

1¼″

8. Stitch gathering threads ⅛″ and ¼″ from both long edges of the strip for the shirred toe. Gather the strip until it measures 4¾″. With right sides together, match one gathered raw edge of the shirred strip to the line on the toe (see pattern). Pin and stitch. Fold the strip over the toe, keeping the gathers smooth (Diagram 2). Baste; trim the shirred strip to match the toe.

Diagram 2

9. Using ¹⁄₁₆″-wide red ribbon and a large-eyed needle, sew a running stitch through the Linda to mark toe and heel lines (see pattern).

10. Baste corresponding pieces of fleece to the wrong side of the front and back of the Linda stocking.

11. With the right sides of the stocking front and back together, stitch, leaving the top edge open. Trim the fleece close to the stitching. Clip the curved seam allowances and turn. Remove any basting.

12. Stitch the stocking lining pieces right sides together, but leave the top edge and area above the heel open (see pattern).

13. With the right sides of the stocking and the stocking lining together, stitch the top edge. Trim seam allowance and turn through the opening above the heel. Slipstitch the opening closed.

14. Tuck the lining inside the stocking with ⅛″ extending above the Linda; pin. Topstitch around the top edge of the stocking on the seam line, using white thread on the spool and blue thread on the bobbin.

15. To make a loop, cut one 6″ length of each color of ribbon. Handling both lengths as one, fold in half and tack the ends 1″ inside the stocking on the right side. Use the remaining ribbons to make bows, and tack the bows to the stocking.

opening for lining

Stocking Pattern

Shirred Toe

77

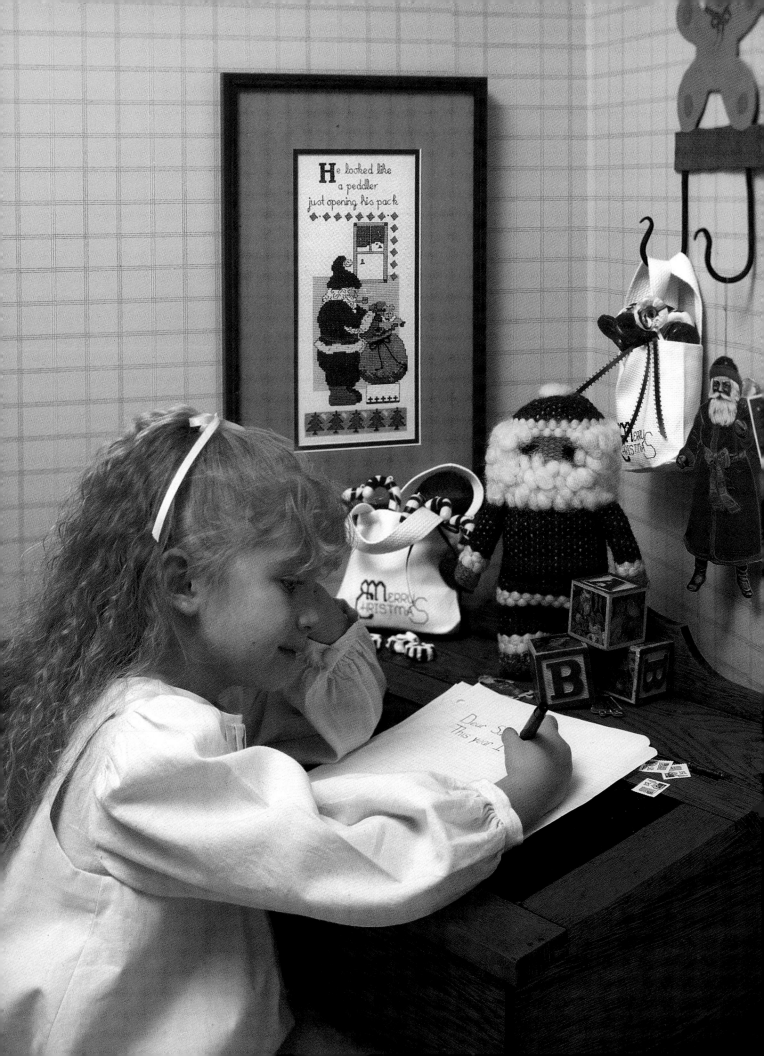

He looked like a peddler just opening his pack...

Peek into Santa's pack of cross-stitch designs and discover the perfect gifts for family and friends. Pick from pillows and picture frames, tote bags and towels—all gifts that will delight the receiver long after Santa's Christmas delivery is past.

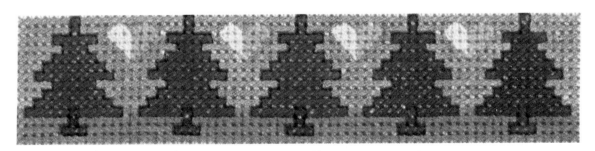

Stitch Count: 156 x 65

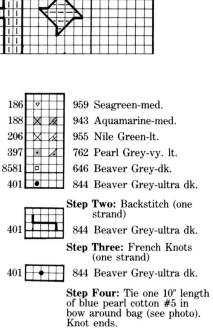

He Looked Like a Peddler

"Dressed all in fur from his head to his foot," this cross-stitched St. Nicholas will be fun to pull out of your Christmas pack every year.

SAMPLE

Stitched on white Linda 27 over two threads, the finished design size is 4¾″ x 11½″. The fabric was cut 11″ x 18″. Finished design sizes using other fabrics are Aida 11—5⅞″ x 14⅛″; Aida 14—4⅝″ x 11⅛″; Aida 18—3⅝″ x 8⅝″; Hardanger 22—3″ x 7⅛″.

SUSAN BATES			DMC (used for sample)
			Step One: Cross-stitch (two strands)
1	·	◿	White
295	+	◿	726 Topaz-lt.
306	−	◿	725 Topaz
778	∴	◿	754 Peach Flesh-lt.
8	s	◿	353 Peach Flesh
49	■	◿	3689 Mauve-lt.
970	z		315 Antique Mauve-dk.
59	▬		326 Rose-vy. deep
44	o		816 Garnet
44	∴		814 Garnet-dk.
104	I	◿	210 Lavender-med.
101	△	◿	327 Antique Violet-dk.
121	o	◿	793 Cornflower Blue-med.
940	▲		792 Cornflower Blue-dk.
119	+		333 Blue Violet-dk.
186	▽		959 Seagreen-med.
188	⊠	◿	943 Aquamarine-med.
206	⊠	◿	955 Nile Green-lt.
397	·	◿	762 Pearl Grey-vy. lt.
8581	□		646 Beaver Grey-dk.
401	●		844 Beaver Grey-ultra dk.

Step Two: Backstitch (one strand)

401		844 Beaver Grey-ultra dk.

Step Three: French Knots (one strand)

401	●	844 Beaver Grey-ultra dk.

Step Four: Tie one 10″ length of blue pearl cotton #5 in bow around bag (see photo). Knot ends.

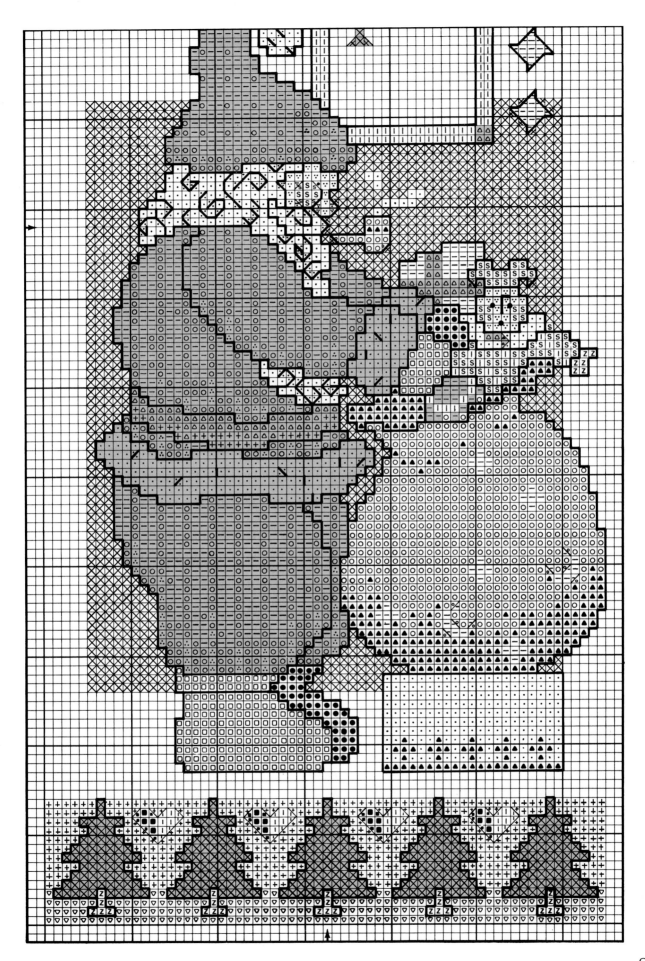

81

Stitch Count: 41 x 40

Stitch Count: 41 x 40

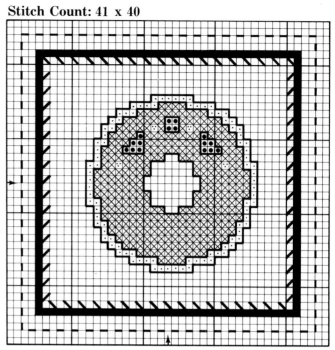

Ruffled Pillows

Colorful ribbons and shiny beads accent the simple cross-stitch designs on these little ruffled pillows. The beads are sewn over the cross-stitch, and the ribbons are couched along the edges of the design to create a border.

SAMPLE

Stitched on white Aida 11, the finished design size is 3¾" x 3⅝". The fabric was cut 8" x 8". Finished design sizes for other fabrics are Aida 14—2⅞" x 2⅞"; Aida 18—2¼" x 2¼"; Hardanger 22—1⅞" x 1⅞".

Heart

MATERIALS

1¾" yards of ¹⁄₁₆"-wide lavender satin ribbon; matching thread
1⅜" yards of ¹⁄₁₆"-wide burgundy satin ribbon; matching thread
Large-eyed needle

SUSAN BATES		DMC (used for sample)
		Step One: Cross-stitch (two strands)
42	·	335 Rose
95	o	554 Violet-lt.
99	X	552 Violet-dk.
		Step Two: Backstitch (one strand)
25		3326 Rose-lt. (running stitch outside design)
401		844 Beaver Grey-ultra dk. (heart)
		Step Three: Beadwork (sewn over cross-stitch)
	o	Light Purple
	X	Dark Purple

Step Four: Ribbonwork

Tack all ribbon ends on the wrong side of the stitched piece.

Stitch with light lavender ribbon.

Lay the light lavender ribbon in place, threading the ribbon ends to the wrong side. Couch diagonally with burgundy ribbon.

Cut one 6" length of burgundy ribbon. Fold the ribbon in half. Tack the fold to the center of the cross-stitch heart. Thread ribbon ends to the wrong side and tack the ribbon in place across the heart (see photo). Tie a small bow with the remaining burgundy ribbon. Tack it to the center of the heart.

Wreath

MATERIALS

2 yards of ¹⁄₁₆"-wide turquoise satin ribbon; matching thread
1 yard of ¹⁄₁₆"-wide white satin ribbon
Large-eyed needle

SUSAN BATES		DMC (used for sample)
		Step One: Cross-stitch (two strands)
292	·:	3078 Golden Yellow-vy. lt.
8	·	761 Salmon-lt.
9	X	760 Salmon
20	●	498 Christmas Red-dk.
		Step Two: Backstitch (one strand)
20		498 Christmas Red-dk. (running stitch outside design)
401		844 Beaver Grey-ultra dk. (wreath)
		Step Three: Beadwork (sewn over cross-stitch)
	·:	White
	●	Red
	●	Red (heart-shaped bead glued over cross-stitch)

Step Four: Ribbonwork

Tack all ribbon ends on the wrong side of the stitched piece.

Stitch with turquoise ribbon.

Lay turquoise ribbon in place, threading ends to wrong side. Couch diagonally with white ribbon.

Stitch the turquoise ribbon over the lower right side of the cross-stitch wreath three times (see photo). Tie a small bow with the remaining turquoise ribbon. Tack it to the lower right side of the wreath.

continued

Stitch Count: 41 x 40

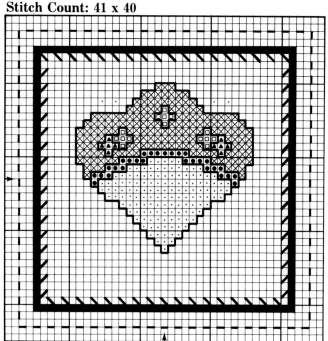

Stitch Count: 41 x 40

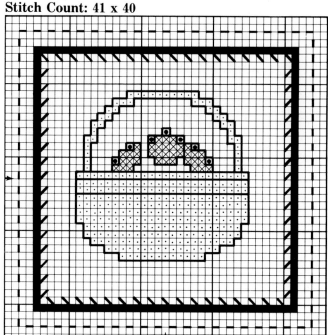

Fan

MATERIALS

1⅝ yards of ¹⁄₁₆″-wide yellow satin
 ribbon; matching thread
1 yard of ¹⁄₁₆″-wide light lavender
 satin ribbon
⅝ yard of ¹⁄₁₆″-wide dark lavender
 satin ribbon; matching thread
Large-eyed needle

SUSAN BATES		DMC (used for sample)
		Step One: Cross-stitch (two strands)
292	·	3078 Golden Yellow-vy. lt.
20	▢	498 Christmas Red-dk.
98	▲	553 Violet-med.
167	✕	519 Sky Blue
168	●	518 Wedgewood-lt.
		Step Two: Backstitch (one strand)
98		553 Violet-med. (running stitch outside design)
401		844 Beaver Grey-ultra dk. (fan)
		Step Three: Beadwork (sewn over cross-stitch)
	·	Yellow
	▢	Red
	▲	Purple
		Step Four: Ribbonwork
		Tack all ribbon ends on the wrong side of the stitched piece.

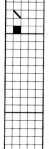

Stitch with yellow ribbon.

Lay the yellow ribbon in place, threading the ends to the wrong side. Couch diagonally with light lavender ribbon.

Stitch across the bottom yellow portion of fan three times, using dark lavender ribbon and tacking in place (see photo). Tie a small bow with the remaining dark lavender ribbon. Tack it to the bottom of the fan.

Basket

MATERIALS

2½ yards of ¹⁄₁₆″-wide peach satin
 ribbon; matching thread
1 yard of ¹⁄₁₆″-wide rust satin
 ribbon
One 5″ length of ⅛″-wide orange
 grosgrain ribbon
Large-eyed needle

SUSAN BATES		DMC (used for sample)
		Step One: Cross-stitch (two strands)
347	·	402 Mahogany-vy. lt.
20	●	498 Christmas Red-dk.
168	✕	518 Wedgewood-lt.
		Step Two: Backstitch (one strand)
168		518 Wedgewood-lt. (running stitch outside design)
401		844 Beaver Grey-ultra dk. (basket)

Step Three: Beadwork (sewn over cross-stitch)

| | · | Red |

Step Four: Ribbonwork

Tack all ribbon ends on the wrong side of the stitched piece.

Stitch with peach ribbon.

Lay the peach ribbon in place, threading the ends to the wrong side. Couch diagonally with rust ribbon.

Tack the orange ribbon across the basket between the backstitch lines.

Stitch the peach ribbon diagonally over the cross-stitch basket handle. Tie a small bow with the remaining ribbon. Tack it to the right side of the handle.

MATERIALS for pillow

Completed cross-stitch on white
 Aida 11; see sample information
¼ yard of 45″-wide white fabric;
 matching thread
2½ yards of ⅛″-wide satin ribbon
Floss to match ribbon
Stuffing

DIRECTIONS

1. From Aida, cut one 6″ square with the design centered.

2. From white fabric, cut one 6″ square for the back. Also cut four 3″ x 10″ strips for ruffles.

3. Fold ½″ of the short edges of the white strips to the wrong side and press. Fold the four strips in half lengthwise to measure 1½″ x 9″ and press. Stitch gathering threads along the 9″ edge, and gather to 5″.

4. Using two strands of floss, sew a running stitch ¼″ from the fold of each ruffle.

5. With right sides together, pin one ruffle to each side of the Aida, matching the raw edges and centering the ruffle ½″ from each corner. Stitch with a ½″ seam.

6. With right sides together and the ruffle sandwiched between, stitch the pillow front and back to one another with a ½″ seam. Leave a 2″ opening on one side. Turn.

7. Stuff the pillow firmly. Slip-stitch the opening closed.

8. Cut the ribbon into four equal lengths. Tie each length into a double bow and tack it to the corners of the pillow.

Jar Covers and Bands

Dress up homemade gifts from your kitchen with decorative covers and bands for canning jars. If you are short on time, fill the jars with nuts, candy, or even popcorn.

SAMPLE
Stitched on white Aida 14, the finished design size is 1¼″ x 1¼″. The fabric was cut 12″ x 12″. Finished design sizes using other fabrics are Aida 11—1½″ x 1½″; Aida 14—1¼″ x 1¼″; Aida 18—1″ x 1″; Hardanger 22—¾″ x ¾″.

SAMPLE
Stitched on white Aida 18, the finished design size for one motif is 1″ x 1″. The fabric was cut 4″ x the jar's circumference plus another 4″. The motifs were centered vertically and repeated as desired.

Flowers

SUSAN BATES		DMC (used for samples)

Step One: Cross-stitch (two strands) or beadwork

366	=	951	Sportsman Flesh-vy. lt./Yellow Bead
8	o	761	Salmon-lt./Light Pink Bead
104	X	210	Lavender-med./Light Lavender Bead
189	●	991	Aquamarine-dk./Dark Green Bead

Step Two: Backstitch (one strand)/Not done with beadwork

| 401 | | 844 | Beaver Grey-ultra dk. |

Stitch Count: 17 x 17

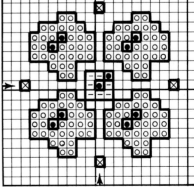

continued 85

Stitch Count: 17 x 17

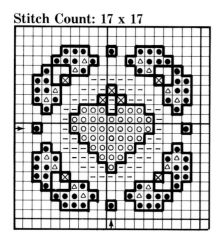

Heart

SUSAN BATES		DMC (used for sample)	
		Step One: Cross-stitch (two strands)or beadwork	
871	o	3041	Antique Violet-med./Lavender Bead
215	△	369	Pistachio Green-vy. lt./Light Green Bead
189	●	991	Aquamarine-dk./Dark Green Bead
885	–	739	Tan-ultra vy. lt./Cream Bead
362	☒	437	Tan-lt./Yellow Bead
		Step Two: Backstitch (one strand)/Not done with beadwork	
401		844	Beaver Grey-ultra dk.

Jar Cover

MATERIALS

Completed beadwork on white
 Aida; see sample information
Tracing paper for pattern
One 11″ x 11″ piece of white fabric;
 matching thread
1 yard of ⅜″-wide satin ribbon

DIRECTIONS

1. Make a 9″ circle pattern (see Appendix).

2. From Aida with beadwork, cut one circle with the design centered.

3. From the white fabric, cut one circle.

4. Stitch the right sides of the circle pieces together, leaving a 3″ opening. Clip the seam allowances and turn. Slipstitch the opening closed and press.

5. Place the cover on jar and tie a ribbon in a bow around the cover.

Jar Band

MATERIALS

Completed cross-stitch on white
 Aida; see sample information
Tracing paper for pattern
One 14″ x 14″ piece of fabric;
 matching thread
White thread

DIRECTIONS

1. Make a pattern for an 11½″ circle (see Appendix).

2. Cut one circle from the fabric. Fold under the edges of the circle ¼″ two times and stitch.

3. With the design centered, cut one piece of Aida 3″ x jar's circumference plus another 2″.

4. Press under 1″ of the bottom edge of the Aida. Press the top edge under ½″ two times and slipstitch to the bottom edge. Fold the raw ends of the strip to the inside.

5. Place the fabric over the jar and place the cross-stitch band around the jar to hold the fabric in place. Insert one end of the band inside the opposite end until it is tight around jar. Slipstitch it to hold it in place.

A Christmas Goose

Irregular patterns of color, shaping the wing and feathers in the Christmas goose, give it the appearance of a colorful cross-stitch mosaic. A little glass heart, hung like a medallion around its neck, and tiny beads add sparkle to the design.

SAMPLE

Stitched on cream Aida 14, the finished design size is 6¼″ x 4⅞″. The fabric was cut 13″ x 11″. Finished design sizes using other fabrics are Aida 11—7⅞″ x 6⅛″; Aida 18—4⅞″ x 3¾″; Hardanger 22—4″ x 3⅛″.

SUSAN BATES		DMC (used for sample)	
		Step One: Cross-stitch (two strands)	
292	•	3078	Golden Yellow-vy. lt.
292	U	3078	Golden Yellow-vy. lt. (bead over cross-stitch)
894	–	223	Shell Pink-med.
47	I	304	Christmas Red-med.
43	☒	815	Garnet-med.
849	o	927	Grey Green-med.
849	s	927	Grey Green-med. (bead over cross-stitch)
851	■	924	Grey Green-vy. dk.
851	▲	924	Grey Green-vy. dk. (bead over cross-stitch)
		Step Two: Backstitch (two strands)	
849		927	Grey Green-med.
		Step Three: Beadwork	
	U		Light Yellow
	s		Grey Green
	▲		Dark Green
	□		Light Blue Heart Bead—Glue bead in place.

Stitch Count: 87 x 68

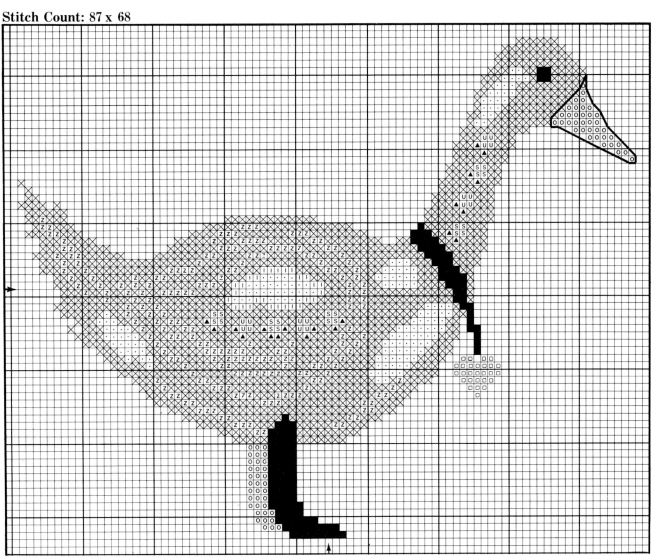

Left to right: Christmas Preserves,
Cinnamon Bear Bag, Christmas
Towel, Chocolate Kiss Bag.

Sweet Temptations

Gifts of Christmas candies, packaged in clever cross-stitch bags, are a sweet temptation for children of all ages during the holiday season (see photo, page 88).

Cinnamon Bear Bag

SAMPLE

Stitched on white Hardanger 22 over one thread, the finished design size for the bag is 5½" x ⅞". The fabric was cut 9" x 5". The five bears were centered and stitched seven thread units apart. Finished design sizes for one motif using other fabrics are Aida 11—1¾" x 1¾"; Aida 14—1⅜" x 1⅜"; Aida 18—1" x 1".

SUSAN BATES	DMC (used for sample)
	Step One: Cross-stitch (one strand)
46	666 Christmas Red-bright

MATERIALS

Completed cross-stitch on white Hardanger; see sample information
¼ yard of 45"-wide red print fabric; matching thread
¼ yard of 45"-wide solid fabric for lining; matching thread
2 yards of ⅛"-wide white satin ribbon
14 red wooden beads or discs

Stitch Count: 19 x 19

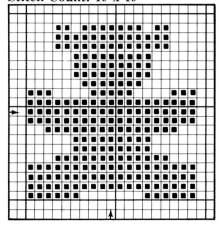

DIRECTIONS

1. From Hardanger, cut one 2½" x 7" piece with the design centered.

2. From the print fabric, cut one 7" x 10½" piece for the back. Also cut one 5" x 7" piece and one 4" x 7" piece for the front.

3. From solid fabric, cut two 7" x 10½" pieces for lining.

4. With right sides together, stitch the 5" x 7" print fabric piece to top edge of the Hardanger with ¼" seam. Sew the 4" x 7" print fabric piece to the bottom edge of Hardanger to complete the bag front.

5. With right sides together, stitch the sides and bottom of the front and back to one another with a ¼" seam.

6. Fold the corner so that the side seam and bottom seam meet; stitch (Diagram). Repeat with the second corner.

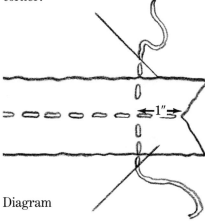

Diagram

7. Repeat Steps 5 and 6 with the lining pieces, leaving a 2" opening on one side.

8. With right sides together, slide the lining over the bag, matching side seams. Stitch around the top edge of the bag with a ¼" seam. Turn and stuff the lining inside the bag. Press.

9. To make the casing, stitch 1½" below and parallel to the top edge of the bag. Stitch again ½" below and parallel to the first row of stitching. Between rows of stitching, snip side seams of outer fabric.

10. Cut the ribbon into two equal lengths. Thread the ribbon into the opening on one side, through casing, and out the same opening. Thread the second ribbon in and out of the opening on the opposite side.

11. Thread wooden beads or discs onto the ribbon; then knot the ribbon to hold them in place.

Chocolate Kiss Bag

SAMPLE

Stitched on white Aida 14, the finished design size for one motif is ¾" x 1¾". The fabric was cut 9" x 5". The five motifs are centered and stitched four thread units apart. Finished design sizes for one motif using other fabrics are Aida 11—1" x 2¼"; Aida 18—⅝" x 1⅜"; Hardanger 22—½" x 1⅛".

SUSAN BATES	DMC (used for sample)
	Step One: Cross-stitch (three strands)
360	898 Coffee Brown-vy. dk.
46	666 Christmas Red-bright

Stitch Count: 25 x 11

Stitch Count: 29 x 18

 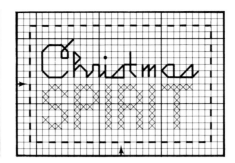 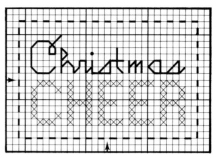

MATERIALS

Completed cross-stitch on white
  Aida; see sample information
¼ yard of 45″-wide brown print
  fabric; matching thread
¼ yard of 45″-wide red print fabric
  for lining; matching thread
2 yards ⅛″-wide white satin ribbon
12 red wooden beads or discs

DIRECTIONS

1. From Aida, cut one 2¾″ x 6″
piece with the design centered.

2. From the brown print fabric, cut
one 6″ x 13″ piece for the back. Also
cut one 6″ x 7½″ and one 6″ x 3½″
piece for the front.

3. From the red print fabric, cut
two 6″ x 13″ pieces for the lining.

4. With right sides together, stitch
the 6″ x 7½″ brown fabric piece to
the top edge of the Aida with a ¼″
seam. Sew the 6″ x 3½″ brown fabric
piece to the bottom edge of the Aida
to complete the bag front.

5. Repeat Steps 5 through 9 of the
Cinnamon Bear Bag, cutting the
threads in the right seam only.

6. Cut the ribbon into two equal
lengths. Handling both ribbons as
one, thread into the opening and
through the casing.

7. Thread wooden beads or discs
onto ribbon; then knot the ribbon to
hold them in place.

Christmas Preserves

Preserve the spirit, joy, and
cheer of Christmas in soft-sculpture
jars. Hand-crafted accessories add a
special touch to your table or kitchen
counter during the holidays (see
photo, page 88).

SAMPLE

Stitched on white Hardanger 22
over two threads, finished design
size is 2⅝″ x 1⅝″. Fabric was cut 8″ x
7″. Finished design sizes using other
fabrics are Aida 11—2⅝″ x 1⅝″; Aida
14—2⅛″ x 1¼″; Aida 18—1⅝″ x 1″;
Hardanger 22—1⅜″ x ⅞″.

SUSAN BATES		DMC (used for sample)
		Step One: Cross-stitch (three strands)
229	⊠	909 Emerald Green-vy. dk.
		Step Two: Backstitch (two strands)
47		321 Christmas Red (broken lines)
229		909 Emerald Green-vy. dk. (lettering)
		Step Three: French Knots (one strand)
229	•	909 Emerald Green-vy. dk.

Quart Jars

MATERIALS

Completed cross-stitch on white
  Hardanger 22; see sample
  information

Tracing paper for patterns
½ yard of 45″-wide print fabric;
  matching thread
⅜ yard of 45″-wide green fabric;
  matching thread
1 yard of ⅜″-wide red grosgrain
  ribbon
White thread
Batting
⅓ cup fine sand
Small funnel
String

DIRECTIONS

1. From the Hardanger, cut one
2½″ x 3½″ piece with the design centered. Zigzag the edges.

2. Make patterns for 3½″ and 10½″
circles (see Appendix).

3. From the print fabric, cut four
3½″ circles. Also cut one 11″ x 17″
piece.

4. From the green fabric, cut two
10½″ circles.

5. From the batting, cut 7″-wide
strips. Roll the strips together in a
bedroll fashion to make a tight bun-
dle, 18″ in circumference. Tie with
string and set aside.

6. To make weights for the bottom
of the jar, stitch the wrong sides of
two print circles together. Stitch
close to the edge, leaving a 1″ opening. Place a funnel in the opening
and fill nearly full with sand. Stitch
the opening closed and set aside.

continued **91**

7. Fold the 11" x 17" print piece in half with right sides together. Stitch along the 11" edges with a ¼" seam.

8. Fold ¼" to the wrong side along the bottom edge. Sew a running stitch close to the fold with a double strand of matching thread. Gather until you have a 2"-wide opening; knot securely.

9. Fold ½" to the wrong side along the top edge. Sew a running stitch close to the fold with a double strand of matching thread; secure the end but do not cut or gather the thread.

10. Add another running stitch 1" from the top edge. Again, do not cut the thread or gather it.

11. Begin filling the jar, by placing one 3½" circle in the bottom with the wrong side up. Place the sandbag over the circle. Remove the string from the batting and place it in the jar.

12. Draw up the gathering thread that is 1" from the top to make a 3"-wide opening; knot securely. Force the batting below this line; then stuff the jar top with additional batting. Draw up the top gathering thread to form a second 3"-wide opening. Place a second 3½" fabric circle inside the top gathering. Slipstitch over the gathered edge, adjusting the tension of the circle so it is smooth.

13. With the right sides of two 10½" circles together, stitch with a ¼" seam, leaving a 2" opening. Clip the seam allowance and turn. Slipstitch the opening closed.

14. Sew a running stitch 2" from the outside edge with a double strand of matching thread. Place the circle over the jar top and gather it tightly; knot securely. Tack the circle to the jar on the gathering line.

15. Fold ¼" to wrong side of the Hardanger; press. Center on the jar front and slipstitch in place.

16. Tie a ribbon around the jar lid over the gathering lines.

Pint Jars

MATERIALS
Completed cross-stitch on white Hardanger 22; see sample information
Tracing paper for patterns
¼ yard of 45"-wide print fabric; matching thread
¼ yard of 45"-wide green fabric; matching thread
1 yard of ⅜"-wide red grosgrain ribbon
White thread
Batting
⅓ cup fine sand
Small funnel
String

DIRECTIONS
1. From Hardanger, cut one 2½" x 3½" piece with the design centered. Zigzag the edges.

2. Make patterns for 3½" and 8½" circles (see Appendix).

3. From the print fabric, cut four 3½" circles. Also cut one 8" x 14" piece.

4. From the green fabric, cut two 8½" circles. From batting, cut 5"-wide strips. Roll together in bedroll fashion to make a tight cylinder, 13" in circumference. Tie with string and set aside.

5. Complete Steps 6 and 7 of the Quart Jar, sewing the 8" sides.

6. Complete the remainder of the Quart Jar instructions, making allowances for the smaller size.

Stitch Count: 27 x 27

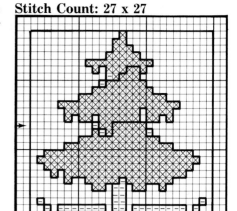

Christmas Towel

Reminiscent of old-fashioned kitchen toweling, this special Hardanger provides a decorative grid to capture favorite Christmas motifs (see photo, page 89).

SAMPLE
Stitched on red kitchen Hardanger 22 over one thread, the finished design size for each motif is 1¼" x 1¼". The fabric was cut 18" x 38". The motifs are stitched on one end of the towel. The edges of the towel were folded under ¼" twice and stitched with matching thread.

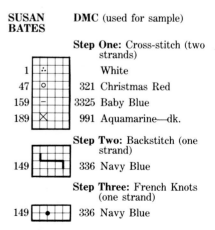

SUSAN BATES		DMC (used for sample)
	Step One: Cross-stitch (two strands)	
1		White
47		321 Christmas Red
159		3325 Baby Blue
189		991 Aquamarine—dk.
	Step Two: Backstitch (one strand)	
149		336 Navy Blue
	Step Three: French Knots (one strand)	
149		336 Navy Blue

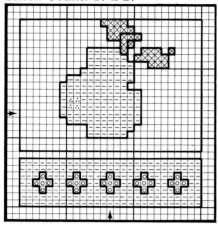

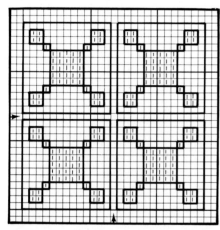

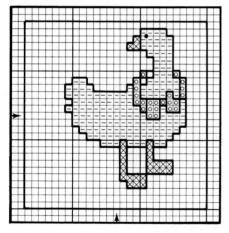

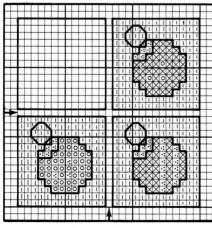

Tea Towel

Flower-filled baskets dance across this Hardanger towel. The crocheted edges add a decorative finish and a delicate touch (see photo, page 95).

SAMPLE

Stitched on cream Hardanger 22 over two threads, the finished design size for the towel is 13⅛" x 2¾". The fabric was cut 16½" x 34". The design was centered horizontally and stitched along the 16½" edge 2" above the edge. The motif was repeated seven times with two thread units between each motif. Finished design sizes for one motif using other fabrics are Aida 11—1¾" x 2¾"; Aida 14—1⅜" x 2⅛"; Aida 18—1⅛" x 1⅝"; Hardanger 22—⅞" x 1⅜".

SUSAN BATES		DMC (used for sample)
		Step One: Cross-stitch (three strands)
366	X	951 Sportsman flesh-vy. lt.
74	-	3354 Dusty Rose-lt.
42	∴	3350 Dusty Rose-vy. dk.
160	o	813 Blue-lt.
161	●	826 Blue-med.
189	□	991 Aquamarine-dk.
362	■	437 Tan-lt.
		Step Two: Backstitch (one strand)
401		844 Beaver Grey-ultra dk.

MATERIALS

Completed cross-stitch on cream
  Hardanger; see sample
  information
Cream thread
One skein #20 ivory DMC Cebelia
  Crochet Thread
One #8 crochet hook

DIRECTIONS

1. Fold the long edges of the towel under ¼" to the wrong side twice and stitch.

2. Fold the short edges of towel under ½" to the wrong side twice and stitch.

3. Crochet the edges with the right side facing you. **Row 1:** At one end of the towel, single crochet through the fabric and over the hemmed edge; *skip 3 double thread blocks of the Hardanger fabric; then single crochet again. Repeat from * across and fasten off. **Row 2:** Single crochet in the first stitch. *Skip 3 stitches, then work the picot shell as follows in next stitch, **1 double crochet, chain 3, 1 single crochet in third chain from hook, repeat from ** three times; 1 double crochet. Skip 3 stitches, 1 single crochet in next stitch. Repeat from * across; fasten off.

4. Repeat the directions in Step 3 to complete the crocheted edge for the opposite end of the towel.

Stitch Count: 20 x 30

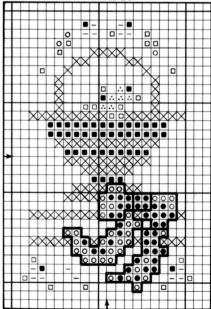

Jewelry Bags

Whether they hold jewelry or potpourri, these little bags will add a feminine touch to your room.

SAMPLE

Stitched on natural Egyptian Cotton Quality D 26 over two threads, the finished design size is 2⅛" x 2¼". The fabric was cut 8" x 17". The top edge of the design was stitched 4½" below the top 8" edge of the fabric and centered horizontally. Finished design sizes using other fabrics are Aida 11—2½" x 2¾"; Aida 14—1⅞" x 2⅛"; Aida 18—1½" x 1⅝"; Hardanger 22—1¼" x 1⅜".

SUSAN BATES		DMC (used for sample)
		Step One: Cross-stitch (two strands)
49	✕	3689 Mauve-lt.
66	o	3688 Mauve-med.
69	▾	3687 Mauve
869	▵	3042 Antique Violet-lt.
101	◎	327 Antique Violet-dk.
128	▦	800 Delft-pale
160	■	813 Blue-lt.
213	◻	369 Pistachio Green-vy. lt.
214	⊣	966 Baby Green-med.
876	✕	502 Blue Green
942	·	738 Tan-vy. lt.
362	∴	437 Tan-lt.
		Step Two: Backstitch (one strand)
150		823 Navy Blue-dk.
		Step Three: French Knots (one strand)
150	●	823 Navy Blue-dk.

MATERIALS

Completed cross-stitch on Glenshee Egyptian Cotton; see sample information

5½" x 15" piece of lightweight fabric for lining; matching thread

¾ yard of ½"-wide cream flat trim; matching thread

1 yard of 1/16"-wide ribbon to match lining

DIRECTIONS

All seam allowances are ¼".

1. From Glenshee, cut one 5½" x 15" piece with the bottom edge of the design 5½" from the top narrow edge of the fabric and centered horizontally. Zigzag the edges.

2. Cut one 16" length of cream trim. Stitch the trim to the Glenshee around the design. Place the outside edge of the trim 1" from the widest point of the design (see photo).

3. Fold the Glenshee with right sides together to measure 5½" x 7½". Stitch the side seams. Turn right side out.

4. Fold the lining right sides together to measure 5½" x 7½". Stitch the side seams, leaving a 3" opening.

5. Slide the lining over the Glenshee with right sides together, matching the side seams. Stitch around the top edges. Turn right side out and slipstitch the opening closed. Tuck the lining inside the Glenshee.

6. To make a casing, sew two parallel rows of stitching, one ¾" from the top seam and the other 1" from the top seam. In both side seams of the Glenshee, carefully cut the threads that are between the rows of stitching.

7. Slipstitch the remaining trim to the top edge of the bag.

8. Cut the ribbon into two equal lengths. Thread one ribbon through each casing. Tie the ribbons into small bows on each side of the bag.

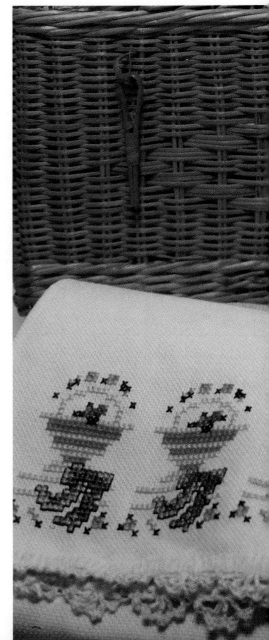

Left to right: Tea Towel, Jewelry Bags.

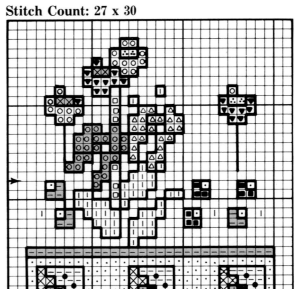

**Left to right: Snowman Pillow,
Gift Bags.**

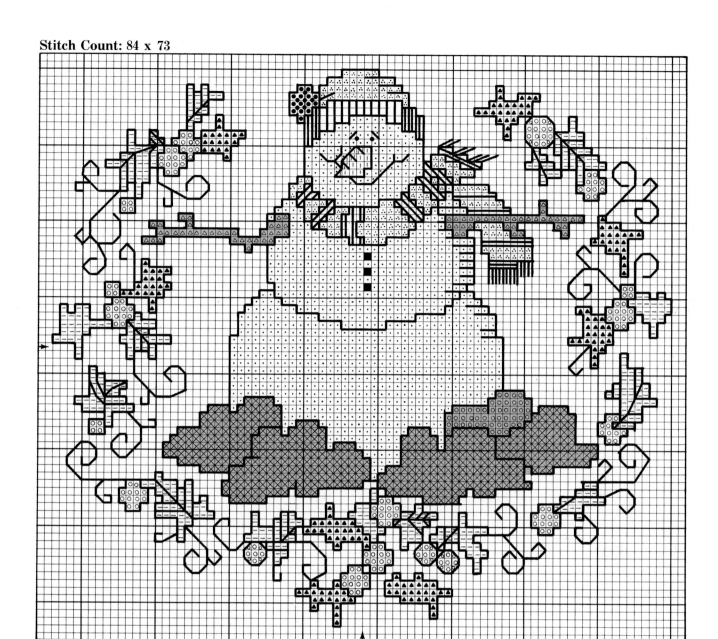

Snowman Pillow

Here's a snowman to enjoy all winter long. Stitched on Hardanger he is guaranteed not to melt.

SAMPLE

Stitched on red Hardanger 22 over two threads, the finished design size is 7⅝" x 6⅝". The fabric was cut 12" x 12". Finished design sizes using other fabrics are Aida 11—7⅝" x 6⅝"; Aida 14—6" x 5¼"; Aida 18—4⅝" x 4"; Hardanger 22—3⅞" x 3⅜".

SUSAN BATES			DMC (used for sample)
			Step One: Cross-stitch (three strands)
1	·	⁄	White
330	ı	⁄	947 Burnt Orange
335	o	⁄	606 Orange Red-bright
158	X		775 Baby Blue-lt.
159	⊙		3325 Baby Blue
134	∴		820 Royal Blue-vy. dk.
256	–		704 Chartreuse-bright
229	▲		909 Emerald Green-vy. dk.
371	△		433 Brown-med.
403	■		310 Black

			Step Two: Backstitch (one strand)
134			820 Royal Blue-vy. dk. (scarf)
403			310 Black (two strands, all else)

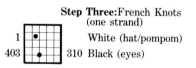

Step Three: French Knots (one strand)

1	•	White (hat/pompom)
403	•	310 Black (eyes)

MATERIALS
Completed cross-stitch on red Hardanger; see sample information
Tracing paper for patterns
½ yard of 45"-wide blue print fabric; matching thread
1¾ yards of small cording
Fusible interfacing
Stuffing
Dressmaker's pen

continued

DIRECTIONS

1. Make a 10″ circle pattern (see Appendix).

2. From Hardanger, cut one circle for the pillow front with the design centered.

3. From the blue print fabric, cut one circle for the pillow back. For the shirring, cut 3″-wide bias strips, piecing as needed, to equal 1½ yards. Also cut 1½″-wide bias strips, piecing as needed, to equal 60″. Cover the cording and cut into two 30″ lengths.

4. From fusible interfacing, cut one circle.

5. Fold the Hardanger circle into quarters and mark. Following manufacturer's instructions, fuse interfacing to wrong side of fabric.

6. Fold the blue print pillow back into quarters and mark.

7. Matching the raw edges of one length of cording to raw edges of the right side of the Hardanger, stitch a ½″ seam. Sew the second length of cording to the pillow back.

8. With right sides of the shirred strip together, stitch a ¼″ seam in the 3″ ends. Fold into quarters and mark both edges. Stitch gathering threads ¼″ and ½″ from both long edges. Gather only one edge to fit circumference of circle.

9. With right sides together, match the quarter marks and raw edges of the shirred strip to the marks on the Hardanger. Stitch a ½″ seam around the circle.

10. Gather the remaining edge of the strip to fit the circumference of circle. Match quarter marks and raw edges of the shirred strip with the right side of the pillow back. Stitch a ½″ seam around the circle, leaving a 4″ opening. Trim and clip the seam allowance. Turn.

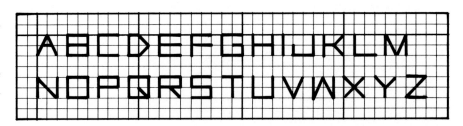

11. Stuff firmly and slipstitch the opening closed.

Gift Bags

A cross-stitcher's approach to Christmas gift wrapping—personalized gift bags (see photo, page 96).

Mitch's Bag

SAMPLE
Stitched on white Aida 14, the finished design size is 1⅞″ x 3¼″. The fabric was cut 8″ x 10″. Finished design sizes using other fabrics are Aida 11—2⅜″ x 4⅛″; Aida 18—1½″ x 2½″; Hardanger 22—1⅛″ x 2″.

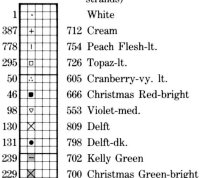

SUSAN BATES		DMC (used for sample)
		Step One: Cross-stitch (two strands)
1	·	White
387	+	712 Cream
778	I	754 Peach Flesh-lt.
295	□	726 Topaz-lt.
50	∴	605 Cranberry-vy. lt.
46	■	666 Christmas Red-bright
98	▽	553 Violet-med.
130	✕	809 Delft
131	●	798 Delft-dk.
239	▬	702 Kelly Green
229	✕	700 Christmas Green-bright
371	○	433 Brown-med.
382	▲	3371 Black Brown
		Step Two: Backstitch (one strand)
46		666 Christmas Red-bright (clown)
46		666 Christmas Red-bright (two strands, candy canes)
382		3371 Black Brown (two strands, name)
382		3371 Black Brown (all else)
		Step Three: French Knots (one strand)
382	◆	3371 Black Brown

Nate's Bag

SAMPLE
Stitched on white Aida 14, the finished design size is 1⅞″ x 3⅝″. The fabric was cut 8″ x 10″. Finished design sizes using other fabrics are Aida 11—2½″ x 4½″; Aida 18—1½″ x 2¾″; Hardanger 22—1¼″ x 2¼″.

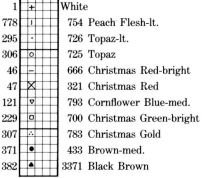

SUSAN BATES		DMC (used for sample)
		Step One: Cross-stitch (two strands)
1	+	White
778	I	754 Peach Flesh-lt.
295	·	726 Topaz-lt.
306	○	725 Topaz
46	—	666 Christmas Red-bright
47	✕	321 Christmas Red
121	▽	793 Cornflower Blue-med.
229	□	700 Christmas Green-bright
307	∴	783 Christmas Gold
371	●	433 Brown-med.
382	▲	3371 Black Brown
		Step Two: Backstitch (one strand)
371		433 Brown-med. (two strands, baseball bat)
382		3371 Black Brown (two strands, name)
382		3371 Black Brown (all else)

MATERIALS
Completed cross-stitch on white Aida 14; see sample information

One 6″ x 8″ piece unstitched white Aida 14 for back; matching thread

Small piece of print fabric for top; matching thread

Small pieces of white fabric for lining

1 yard of ⅜″-wide ribbon to match print fabric

Three ⅜″-wide wooden beads or two large jingle bells

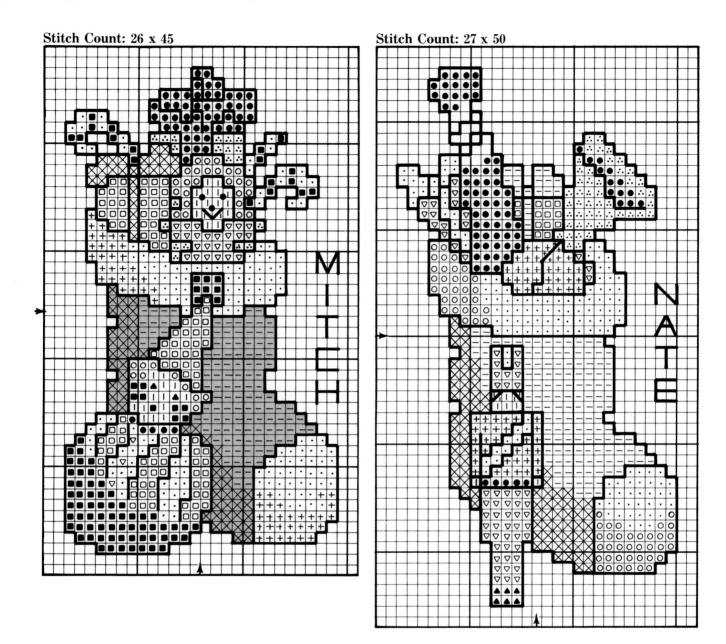

DIRECTIONS

All seam allowances are ¼″.

1. From the stitched Aida, cut one 6″ x 8″ piece, with the design centered horizontally, and the bottom edge of design placed 2″ from the bottom 6″ edge of the fabric.

2. From the print fabric, cut two 6″ squares, for top band.

3. From the white fabric, cut two 6″ x 8″ pieces, for lining.

4. With the right sides of the Aida pieces together, stitch the sides and bottom.

5. With the right sides of the print pieces together, stitch two opposite 6″ edges, forming a tube.

6. With the right sides of two lining pieces together, stitch the sides and bottom, leaving a 3″ opening in the bottom edge.

7. With right sides together, slide the print band for the top over the Aida and match the side seams. Stitch the band to the top edge of the Aida.

8. With right sides together, match the side seams of the open edge of the lining to unstitched edge of the print band and stitch. Turn

through the opening and then slip-stitch the opening closed.

9. Fold the lining inside the bag, with the seam allowances pressed under the band. To make the casing, stitch on the Aida, close to band through all the layers. Stitch again ½″ above and parallel to the first stitching, using green thread.

10. Carefully cut the threads in the right side seam, between the stitching lines of the casing. Thread the ribbon through the casing and tie beads or bells onto the ribbon.

Little Tote Bags

Filled with peppermints and chocolates, these little totes become perfect party favors for all your special holiday guests.

Chocolate Kisses with Green Heart

SAMPLE (see graph, page 90)
Stitched on white Aida 14, the finished design size is 5¼" x 1⅞". The fabric was cut 15½" x 8½". The first motif was begun 2¾" from the left 8½" edge and 5" from the top 15½" edge. Five motifs were stitched horizontally, with motifs spaced 5 thread units apart. The fourth heart in the row was stitched with DMC 909 Emerald Green-vy. dk.

Merry Christmas

SAMPLE (see photo, page 78)
Stitched on white Aida 14, the finished design size is 3¼" x 1⅝". The fabric was cut 15½" x 8½". The stitching begins 4" from the left 8½" edge and 5¼" from the top 15½" edge. Finished design sizes using other fabrics are Aida 11—4⅛" x 2"; Aida 18—2½" x 1¼"; Hardanger 22—2⅛" x 1".

SUSAN BATES		DMC (used for sample)
		Step One: Cross-stitch (two strands)
20/879	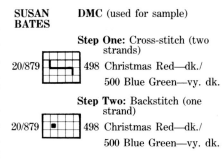	498 Christmas Red—dk./ 500 Blue Green—vy. dk.
		Step Two: Backstitch (one strand)
20/879		498 Christmas Red—dk./ 500 Blue Green—vy. dk.

Bah Humbug!

SAMPLE
Stitched on white Aida 14, the finished design size is 1⅞" x 1⅝". The fabric was cut 15½" x 8½". The stitching was begun 6" from the left 8½" edge and 5½" from the 15½" top edge. Finished design sizes for other fabrics are Aida 11—2¼" x 2"; Aida 18—1⅜" x 1¼"; Hardanger 22—1⅛" x 1".

SUSAN BATES		DMC (used for sample)
		Step One: Backstitch (one strand)
20	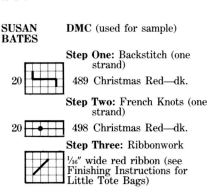	489 Christmas Red—dk.
		Step Two: French Knots (one strand)
20		498 Christmas Red—dk.
		Step Three: Ribbonwork
		⅟₁₆" wide red ribbon (see Finishing Instructions for Little Tote Bags)

Merry Kissmas!

SAMPLE (see graph, page 90)
Stitched on white Aida 14, the finished design size is 5¼" x 3¼". The fabric was cut 15½" x 8½". Begin stitching the chocolate kiss and heart motifs 2¾" from the left 8½" edge of Aida and 5" from the top 15½" edge. The five motifs were stitched horizontally, motifs spaced 5 thread units apart. The lettering is stitched 6" from the left 8½" edge of the Aida and 3¾" from the top edge. Finished design sizes for lettering using other fabrics are Aida 11—2¾" x 1¼"; Aida 18—1¾" x ¾"; Hardanger 22—1⅜" x ⅝".

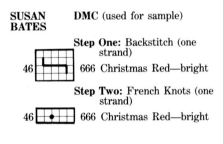

SUSAN BATES	DMC (used for sample)

Step One: Backstitch (one strand)

46 — 666 Christmas Red—bright

Step Two: French Knots (one strand)

46 — 666 Christmas Red—bright

Ho! Ho! Ho!

SAMPLE
Stitched on white Aida 14, the finished design size is 3¾" x 1". The fabric was cut 15½" x 8½". The stitching begins 4" from the left 8½" edge and 6¼" from the top 15½" edge. Finished design sizes using other fabrics are Aida 11—4¾" x 1⅛"; Aida 18—2⅞" x ¾"; Hardanger 22—2⅜" x ⅝".
Also needed: ⅜ yard of 1/16"-wide red satin ribbon
Large-eyed needle

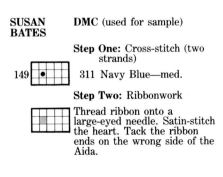

SUSAN BATES	DMC (used for sample)

Step One: Cross-stitch (two strands)

149 — 311 Navy Blue—med.

Step Two: Ribbonwork

Thread ribbon onto a large-eyed needle. Satin-stitch the heart. Tack the ribbon ends on the wrong side of the Aida.

Stitch Count: 46 x 22

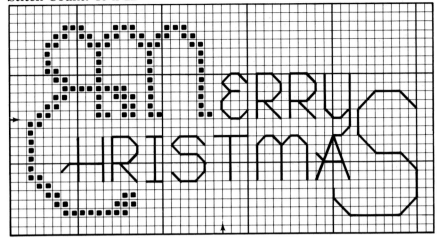

Stitch Count: 25 x 22

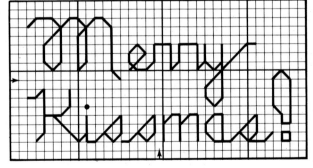

Stitch Count: 31 x 14

Stitch Count: 52 x 13

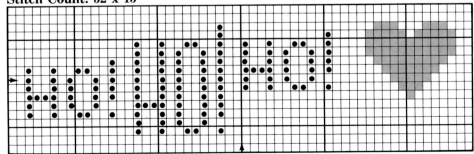

continued **101**

MATERIALS

Completed cross-stitch on white Aida; see sample information 13½" x 6¼" piece of white fabric for lining; matching thread ½ yard of 1"-wide webbing for handle

DIRECTIONS

1. From Aida, cut one 13½" x 6¼" piece. Position the lower edge of the design 1¾" from the 13½" bottom edge of fabric. The following measurements give the distance of the left side of the design from the 6¼" edge:

    Merry Kissmas!—¾"
    Merry Christmas—2"
    Bah Humbug!—3½"
    Chocolate Kisses—¾"
    Ho! Ho! Ho!—2¼"

2. Cut two 9" lengths of webbing.

3. With right sides together, fold the Aida to measure 6¾" x 6¼". Stitch along the one open side and across the bottom.

4. Align the side seam and bottom seam and stitch across the corner (Diagram 1). Repeat with the second corner.

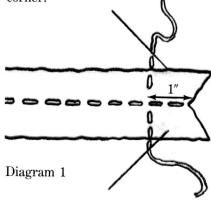

Diagram 1

5. For the "Bah Humbug!" and "Ho! Ho! Ho!" bags, complete the ribbonwork as described in Finishing Options.

6. Repeat Steps 3 and 4 for lining, leaving a 2" opening in the bottom edge.

7. Matching raw edges, pin the webbing to the right sides of the Aida (Diagram 2).

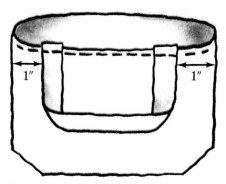

Diagram 2

8. With right sides together and side seams matching, slide the lining over the Aida. Stitch the top edges of the lining and tote bag together. Turn right side out and slipstitch the opening closed.

FINISHING OPTIONS

MERRY KISSMAS!

Materials needed: 1 yard of ⅛"-wide red grosgrain ribbon. Cut the ribbon into two equal lengths. Handling the lengths as one, tie them into a bow around the handle.

MERRY CHRISTMAS (green)

Materials needed: ¾ yard of ¼"-wide burgundy picot-edge satin ribbon. Cut the ribbon into one 10" and one 16" length. Tie the 16" length ribbon into a bow around the handle. Tie the 10" length around the knot of the bow.

MERRY CHRISTMAS (red)

Materials needed: ⅝ yard of ⅛"-wide burgundy satin ribbon; a small piece of burgundy print fabric; a small amount of stuffing; burgundy thread. Cut the ribbon into one 5" length and one 17" length. From the print fabric, cut two hearts (see the heart pattern used with the Angel Stocking and Shepherd Stocking). Stitch them together, leaving a 1" opening. Turn right side out and

stuff. Slipstitch the opening closed. Attach a 5" ribbon length to the heart. Tie a 17" ribbon length into a bow around the handle. Tie ribbon with heart to the knot of the bow.

BAH HUMBUG!

Materials needed: 2 yards of ¹⁄₁₆"-wide green satin ribbon; ½ yard of ¼"-wide red satin ribbon; large-eyed needle. Thread red ribbon onto a large-eyed needle. Stitch the ribbon around the entire bag, tacking the ribbon ends inside the bag. Complete the tote bag. Cut the green ribbon into two equal lengths. Handling ribbon lengths as one, tie them into a bow around the handle.

CHOCOLATE KISSES WITH GREEN HEART

Materials needed: ½ yard of ¼"-wide red satin ribbon. Tie the ribbon into a bow around the handle.

HO! HO! HO!

Materials needed: 1¼ yards of ¹⁄₁₆"-wide red satin ribbon; 1½ yards of ¹⁄₁₆"-wide blue satin ribbon; large-eyed needle. Cut one 11" length of red ribbon for the bow and set aside. Complete the blue and red ribbon borders, following the Ho! Ho! Ho! and ribbonwork graphs. Complete the tote bag. Tie an 11" length of red ribbon in a small bow and tack it to the front of the bag over the red ribbon border.

 Thread ¹⁄₁₆"-wide blue satin ribbon onto a large-eyed needle. Begin stitching at the side seam 1" below the top edge of the bag. Stitch around the entire bag. Tack the ribbon ends inside the bag.

 Thread ¹⁄₁₆"-wide red satin ribbon onto a large-eyed needle. Begin stitching at the side seam 1⅜" below the top edge of the bag. Stitch around the entire bag. Tack the ribbon ends inside bag. Stitch a second red row right below the first (see graph).

Wine Bags

Present your gifts of yuletide "spirits" in these attractive cross-stitched bags. Long after the wine is gone, the bags will still be enjoyed.

SAMPLE

Vertical lettering is stitched using three strands of floss on cream Hardanger 22 over two threads. The fabric was cut 17″ x 17″. The *W* was stitched 5″ from top edge of the fabric and 4″ from the left side. The letters and hearts were spaced two thread units apart (Diagram 1).

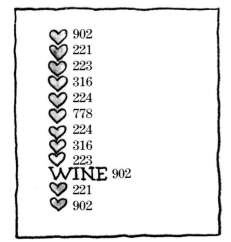

♥	902
♥	221
♥	223
♥	316
♥	224
♥	778
♥	224
♥	316
♥	223
WINE	902
♥	221
♥	902

Diagram 1

SAMPLE

Horizontal lettering is stitched using two strands of floss on cream Hardanger 22 over one thread. The fabric was cut 17″ x 17″. The *W* was stitched 5″ from the bottom edge of the fabric and 4″ from the left side. The letters and hearts were each spaced two thread units apart (Diagram 2).

♥	224
♥	778
♥	224
♥	316
♥	223
WINE	902
♥	221
♥	902

Diagram 2

Stitch Count: 17 x 16

MATERIALS

Completed cross-stitch on cream Hardanger; see sample information
½ yard of 45″-wide dark red fabric for lining; matching thread
½ yard of small cording
2 yards of dark red satin cording for drawstring
Cream thread

DIRECTIONS

1. From Hardanger, cut one 14″ x 15″ piece with the design placed as shown in Diagram 1 or Diagram 2.

2. From dark red fabric, cut one 14″ x 15″ piece for lining. Also cut 1½″-wide bias strips, piecing as needed, to equal 18″ for cording. Cover the cording.

3. Fold the Hardanger, right sides together, to measure 7″ across and 15″ high. Stitch a ½″ seam along the side and across the bottom.

continued

4. Fold the corner so that the side seam lies on top of the bottom seam and forms a triangle. Stitch across the triangle to square the corner (Diagram 3). Repeat with the second corner. Trim seam allowances to ½″.

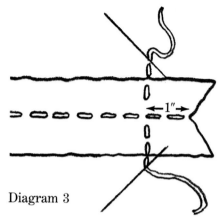

Diagram 3

5. Complete Steps 3 and 4 to make the lining.

6. Turn Hardanger right side out and measure 2½″ from the top edge down the side seam and down the opposite side. Make a ½″ buttonhole below each mark.

7. Stitch the cording to the right side of the Hardanger around the top edge.

8. Slide the lining over the Hardanger, with the right sides together and seams matching. Stitch on the stitching line of the cording, leaving a 3″ opening; turn. Slip the lining inside and slipstitch the opening closed.

9. To make a casing, stitch through all the layers on the top and bottom edge of buttonhole, parallel to the cording.

10. Cut the satin cording into two equal lengths. Thread one length of cording into the opening on one side, through the casing and out the same opening. Repeat with a second length of cording in and out of the second opening. Knot the ends of cording together.

Beaded Soap Bags

Tiny colorful beads form a delicate floral pattern on these scented soap bags. Use other simple cross-stitch graphs to create more beadwork designs to suit your fancy.

SAMPLE

Stitched on white Aida 14, the finished design size is 1⅜" x 1⅜". The fabric was cut 8" x 17". The top edge of the design was stitched 5½" below the top 8" edge of fabric and centered horizontally. Finished design sizes using other fabrics are Aida 11—1¾" x 1¾"; Aida 18—1" x 1"; Hardanger 22—⅞" x ⅞".

Step One: Beadwork

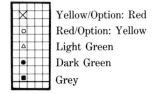

X	Yellow/Option: Red
o	Red/Option: Yellow
△	Light Green
●	Dark Green
■	Grey

MATERIALS

Completed beadwork on white Aida 14; see sample information
5½" x 15" piece of white fabric for lining; matching thread
⅝ yard of ½"-wide white flat lace trim
1¾ yards of 1/16"-wide green satin ribbon
Potpourri

DIRECTIONS

All seam allowances are ¼".

1. From Aida, cut one 5½" x 15" piece with the design centered horizontally. The bottom edge of the design is positioned 4¼" from the top 5½" edge of the Aida. Zigzag all the edges.

2. Cut one 12" length of lace trim. Slipstitch the trim to the Aida with the inside edge of trim ½" from the outside edge of the design (see photo).

3. Fold the Aida with right sides together to measure 5½" x 7½". Stitch the side seams and turn right side out.

4. Fold the lining fabric with right sides together to measure 5½" x 7½". Stitch the side seams, leaving a 3" opening in one side.

5. Slide the lining over the Aida, right sides together and side seams matching. Stitch around the top edge and turn. Slipstitch the opening closed. Tuck the lining inside the Aida.

6. Slipstitch the remaining lace trim to the top edge of the bag.

7. Cut one 28" length of green ribbon and set it aside. Beginning at the corner of the square, thread the remaining ribbon through the lace trim. Tie a bow to secure the ribbon (see photo).

8. Fill the bag with potpourri and tie a 28" length of ribbon around the top of the bag.

Stitch Count: 19 x 19

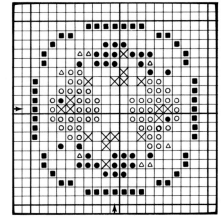

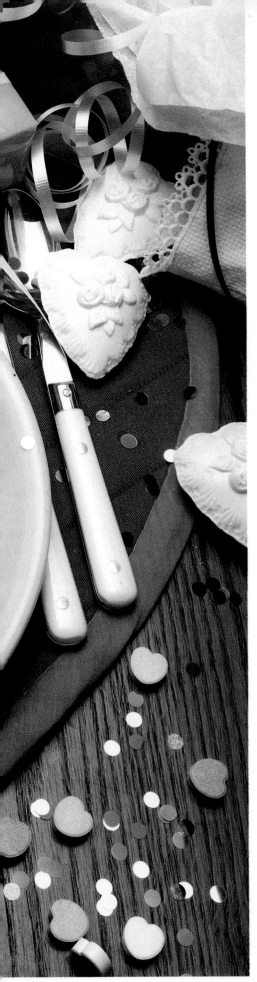

Stitch Count: 36 x 37

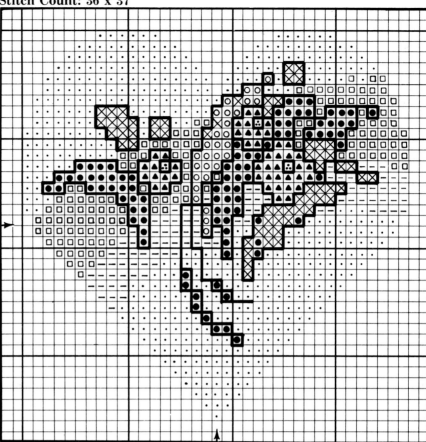

Heart Napkin Rings and Place Mats

For a special late night New Year's Eve dinner for two, decorate your table with these easy-to-make napkin rings and heart-shaped place mats.

SAMPLE

Stitched on white Hardanger 22 over two threads, the finished design size is 3⅜" x 3¼". The fabric was cut 8" x 8". Finished design sizes using other fabrics are Aida 14—2⅝" x 2⅝"; Aida 18—2" x 2"; Hardanger 22—1⅝" x 1⅝".

SUSAN BATES		DMC (used for sample)
		Step One: Cross-stitch (three strands)
293	⁙	727 Topaz-vy. lt.
893	–	224 Shell Pink-lt.
69	▲	3687 Mauve
108	□	211 Lavender-lt.
159	·	827 Blue-vy. lt.
265	✕	3348 Yellow Green-lt.
875	○	503 Blue Green-med.
878	●	501 Blue Green-dk.
		Step Two: Backstitch (one strand)
401		844 Beaver Grey-ultra dk.

Heart Napkin Ring and Place Mat.

place on fold

A

Place Mat Heart Pattern
Match the letters on the two pieces
of the heart to form one pattern.

Napkin Ring

MATERIALS
Completed cross-stitch on white
  Hardanger; see sample
  information
Tracing paper for pattern
One 6″ square piece of unstitched
  white Hardanger; matching
  thread
1¼ yards of ¼″-wide green satin
  ribbon; matching thread
Stuffing

DIRECTIONS
  1. Transfer the pattern for the
napkin ring heart.

  2. From the stitched white Hardanger, cut one heart with the design centered for napkin ring front.
Zigzag the edges.

  3. From the unstitched white Hardanger, cut one heart for the napkin
ring back. Zigzag the edges.

  4. Stitch the right sides of the napkin ring front and back together
with a ¼″ seam, leaving 2″ open on
one side. Carefully clip the curved
seam allowances. Turn. Stuff and
slipstitch the opening closed.

Napkin Ring
Heart Pattern

B

A

5. Cut one 20″ length of ribbon; set aside. Cut the remaining ribbon into two equal lengths. Tack one ribbon length to each side of the heart. Using the 20″ ribbon, tie a bow around the ribbon on the right side of the heart.

Place Mat and Napkin

MATERIALS (for one place mat and napkin)
Tracing paper for pattern
½ yard of 45″-wide green fabric; matching thread
½ yard of 45″-wide pink fabric; matching thread
Polyester batting
Dressmaker's chalk

DIRECTIONS

1. Transfer the pattern for the large heart place mat.

2. From the green fabric, cut two large hearts.

3. From the pink fabric, cut one 15½″ square for the napkin. Also cut 2″-wide bias strips, piecing as needed, to equal 60″.

4. From the polyester batting, cut one large heart.

5. On the flat surface, layer one green heart wrong side up, the batting, and the second green heart right side up. Baste all three layers together. Mark the quilting lines 1¼″ apart on the place mat with dressmaker's chalk (Diagram), and machine-quilt with matching thread. Remove the basting.

Diagram

6. With right sides together and raw edges matching, sew the bias strip around the edge of the front of the place mat with a ½″ seam.

7. Fold the bias strip to the back of the place mat, turn raw edge under and slipstitch.

8. Fold under the edges of the napkins ¼″ twice and stitch.

B

109

Picture Frame

Preserving the spirit of the season in photographs is a tradition for many families. Frame your favorites with the subtle tones of white stitching on cream fabric.

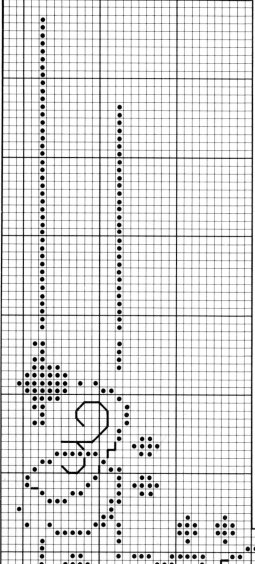

Stitch Count: 82 x 82

SAMPLE

Stitched on Glenshee Egyptian Cotton Quality D 26 over two threads, the finished design size is 6¼" x 6¼". The fabric was cut 12" x 14". Finished design sizes using other fabrics are Aida 11—7½" x 7½"; Aida 14—5⅞" x 5⅞"; Aida 18—4½" x 4½"; Hardanger 22—3¾" x 3¾".

SUSAN BATES	DMC (used for sample)

Step One: Cross-stitch (two strands)

| 1 | • | White |

Step Two: Backstitch (one strand)

| 1 | | White |

MATERIALS

Completed cross-stitch on Glenshee Egyptian Cotton; see sample information
Tracing paper for pattern
One 10" x 12" piece of mat board with a 6½" x 4½" opening for the frame front
One 10" x 12" piece of mat board for the frame back
White glue
Picture hanger

DIRECTIONS

1. Make a pattern for the frame front, using the 10" x 12" mat board with the opening as the pattern.

2. From Glenshee Egyptian Cotton, cut one frame front, adding 2" to the inside and outside edges. Place the design ¾" below and ¾" to the left of the inside opening. Clip the inside corners 1⅞".

3. On a flat surface, layer the Glenshee Egyptian Cotton wrong side up; then put the mat board frame front on top. Make sure the cross-stitch design is in place.

4. Apply a thin line of glue on the mat board around the inside opening. Pull the inside edges of Glenshee Egyptian Cotton through the opening and press down on the glued surface. Make sure the corners are smooth and flat.

5. Apply a thin line of glue on the mat board around the outside edge. Pull up the outside edges of the Glenshee Egyptian Cotton and press down on the glued surface, folding the corners flat.

6. To attach the frame back, apply a thin line of glue around the outside edge on the wrong side of the mat board. Leave a 5¼" opening on the top edge above the center for a photograph. Press the glued surface to the back of frame front.

7. Glue a picture hanger to top center of back.

Merry Christmas
to all and to all a good night.

Merry Christmas to all
and to all a good-night

Merry Christmas! Sing it, shout it—stitch it. With these distinctive holiday designs you will find lots of ways to say it. Stitch a tiny pillow in the shape of an envelope to mail to faraway friends. Give your neighbor a cross-stitched house with its warm Christmas greeting. Hang a wall hanging of Santa and Rudolph or a sweet Nativity scene in your entrance to welcome holiday guests. Each design reflects the warm spirit of the season and says, "Merry Christmas to all."

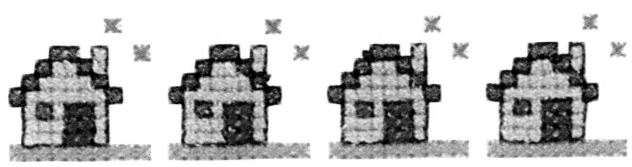

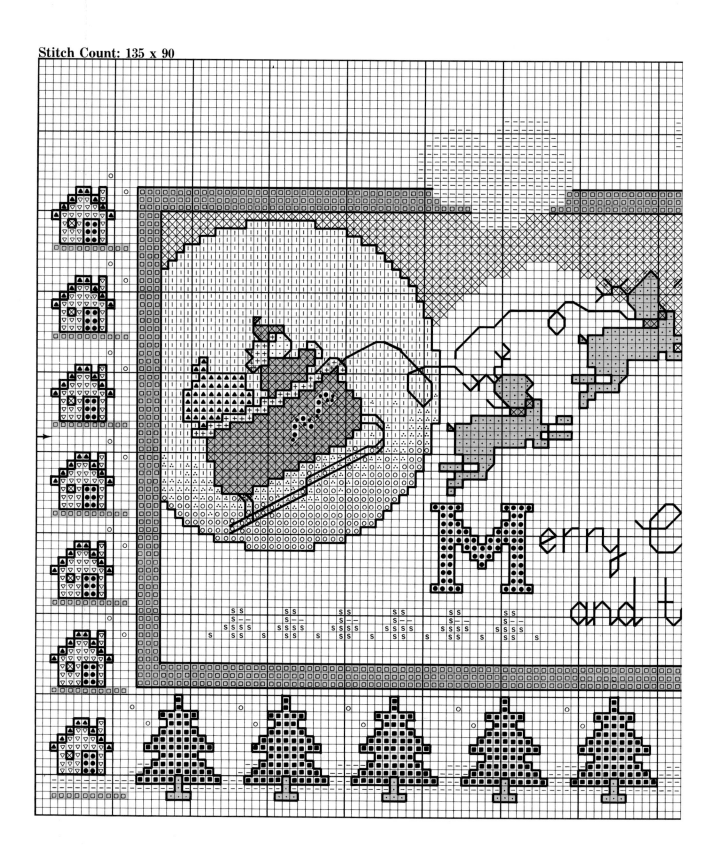

Merry Christmas to All

Stitch St. Nick in his miniature sleigh with three tiny reindeer, to complete your series from *The Night Before Christmas.*

SAMPLE

Stitched on white Linda 27 over two threads, the finished design size is 10″ x 6⅝″. The fabric was cut 16″ x 13″. Finished design sizes using other fabrics are Aida 11—12¼″ x 8⅛″; Aida 14—9⅝″ x 6⅜″; Aida 18—7½″ x 5″; Hardanger 22—6⅛″ x 4⅛″.

SUSAN BATES			DMC (used for sample)

Step One: Cross-stitch (two strands)

1	+	◣		White
293	ı	◿	727	Topaz-vy. lt.
295	∴		726	Topaz-lt.
306	o		725	Topaz
892	·	◿	819	Baby Pink-lt.
893	▽		224	Shell Pink-lt.
59	⊠	◿	326	Rose-vy. deep
108	s		211	Lavender-lt.
101	⊠	◢	327	Antique Violet-dk.
159	–	◿	827	Blue-vy. lt.
147	●	◢	312	Navy Blue-lt.
208	▫		563	Jade-lt.
188	▪		943	Aquamarine-med.
308	▨	◿	782	Topaz-med.
905	▲		645	Beaver Grey-vy. dk.

Step Two: Backstitch (one strand)

401		844 Beaver Grey-ultra dk.

Step Three: French Knot (one strand)

401	•	844 Beaver Grey-ultra dk.

MATERIALS

Completed cross-stitch on white Hardanger; see sample information
Lightweight cardboard for pattern
1 yard of 45″-wide light green fabric; matching thread
One 22″ x 25″ piece of muslin
One 22″ x 24″ piece of bonded batting
Twenty-four ⅜″-wide buttons to be covered
Dressmaker's pen

DIRECTIONS

All seam allowances are ½″.

1. From Hardanger, cut one 12½″ x 15½″ piece, centering the design.

2. From light green fabric, cut one 21″ x 24″ piece for the back. Also cut two 4½″ x 21″ and two 4½″ x 24″ strips for the border and one 1″ x 5″ piece for hanging loops. Cut 2½″-wide bias strips, piecing as needed, to equal 95″.

3. Cover the buttons with the remaining light green fabric, following the manufacturer's instructions.

4. Transfer the holly pattern to cardboard.

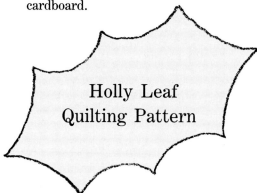

Holly Leaf
Quilting Pattern

5. With right sides together, match the centers of one 4½″ x 24″ strip and one 15½″ side of the Hardanger. Stitch to within ½″ of each edge of the Hardanger.

6. With right sides together, match the centers of one 4½″ x 21″ strip and one 12½″ side of the Hardanger. Stitch to within ½″ of each edge of the Hardanger.

Santa Wall Hanging

In this colorful wall hanging, Santa and Rudolph prepare to make their Christmas Eve deliveries. The quilted holly leaves in the light green border add a seasonal finishing touch.

SAMPLE

Stitched on white Hardanger 22 over two threads, the finished design size is 8⅞″ x 11¼″. The fabric was cut 15″ x 18″. Finished design sizes using other fabrics are Aida 11—8⅞″ x 11¼″; Aida 14—7″ x 8⅞″; Aida 18—5½″ x 6⅞″; Hardanger 22—4½″ x 5⅝″.

SUSAN BATES		DMC (used for sample)	
Step One: Cross-stitch (three strands)			
1	·		White
306	ı	/	725 Topaz
778	−		754 Peach Flesh-lt.
49	□		3689 Mauve-lt.
69	▲		3687 Mauve
70	⊠		3685 Mauve-dk.
76	∴		962 Dusty Rose-med.
47	S		321 Christmas Red
20	⊠	/	498 Christmas Red-dk.
159	⊡		3325 Baby Blue
161	▽	/	826 Blue-med.
186	○	/	993 Aquamarine-lt.
187	E		992 Aquamarine
239	ı		702 Kelly Green
246	■		895 Christmas Green-dk.
362	N		437 Tan-lt.
370	·	/	434 Brown-lt.
400	◻	/	414 Steel Grey-dk.
403	●	◢	310 Black
Step Two: Backstitch (one strand)			
403			310 Black
Step Three: French Knots (one strand)			
403			310 Black

continued

7. To miter the corner, fold the right sides of the corner together and stitch at a 45° angle (Diagram 1). Trim the corner to a ½″ seam allowance; press.

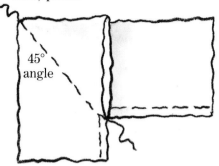

Diagram 1

8. Repeat Steps 5 through 7 to complete the border.

9. Trace the holly pattern onto the border, using a dressmaker's pen.

Draw the remaining pattern freehand (Diagram 2).

10. Place the muslin on a flat surface. Layer the batting over the muslin. Center the front over the batting and muslin. Baste from the center out, following the sequence indicated in Diagram 3.

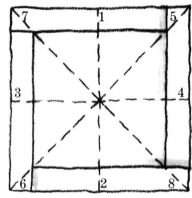

Diagram 3

11. Quilt the pattern by machine or by hand.

12. Place the fabric piece for the back wrong side up on a flat surface. Center the quilted front over the back, right side up. Quilt through all layers, 1″ inside the seams that join the border to the Hardanger (Diagram 2). Also quilt on the Hardanger as close to the seams as possible. Remove basting.

13. Stitch the covered buttons to the wall hanging (Diagram 2).

14. With right sides together, stitch the bias strip to the front of the wall hanging. Begin stitching at the center bottom, ¾″ from the raw edge. Allow for extra fullness at corners. Fold the bias strip in half and then to the back and slipstitch.

15. With right sides together, fold the 1″ x 5″ piece to measure ½″ x 5″. Stitch with a ⅛″ seam and turn. Cut to make two 2½″ pieces. Fold the pieces in half to form loops and tack them to the back of the wall hanging at the corners.

Christmas Envelope

Send Christmas greetings to faraway friends with this tiny envelope pillow.

SAMPLE
Stitched on cream Linda 27 over two threads, the finished design size is 6½″ x 4¾″. The fabric was cut 11″ x 9″. Finished design sizes using other fabrics are Aida 11—8″ x 5¾″; Aida 14—6¼″ x 4⅝″; Aida 18—4⅞″ x 3½″; Hardanger 22—4″ x 2⅞″.

Diagram 2

Stitch Count: 88 x 64

SUSAN BATES		DMC (used for sample)	
		Step One: Cross-stitch (two strands)	
386	−	746	Off-White
968	·	778	Antique Mauve-lt.
969	△	316	Antique Mauve-med.
970	∴	315	Antique Mauve-dk.
72	■	902	Garnet-vy. dk.
779	○	926	Grey Green-dk.
875	I	503	Blue Green-med.
878	✕	501	Blue Green-dk.
355	●	975	Golden Brown-dk.
		Step Two: Backstitch (one strand)	
72		902	Garnet-vy. dk.

continued

MATERIALS

Completed cross-stitch on cream
 Linda; see sample information
One 9½″ x 7½″ piece of unstitched
 cream Linda for envelope back;
 matching thread
⅜ yard of ¾″-wide cream flat trim
 with heart motifs
Stuffing

DIRECTIONS

1. From the stitched Linda, cut
one 9½″ x 7½″ piece, with the design
centered, for the envelope front.

2. Place the trim on the right side
of the unstitched Linda piece in a V
shape to form the flap of the envelope (see photo). Slipstitch the trim
to the Linda.

3. Stitch the right sides of the
Linda pieces together, leaving a 3″
opening on one side. Turn. Stuff the
envelope firmly; then slipstitch the
opening closed.

All Around the House

Simple lines and colors give this
design a fresh contemporary look.
Add a holiday touch by stitching little red beads to the tree, the bushes,
and the holly in the windows.

SAMPLE

Stitched on white Jobelan 28 over
two threads, the finished design size
is 6⅞″ x 7¼″. The fabric was cut 13″
x 13″. Finished design sizes using
other fabrics are Aida 11—8¾″ x
9¼″; Aida 14—6⅞″ x 7¼″; Aida 18—
5⅜″ x 5⅝″; Hardanger 22—4⅜″ x
4⅝″.

SUSAN BATES		DMC (used for sample)
		Step One: Cross-stitch (two strands)
46	○	666 Christmas Red-bright
227	✕	701 Christmas Green-lt.
227	▢	701 Christmas Green-lt. (one strand)
227	∴	701 Christmas Green-lt. (bead over cross-stitch)
403	■	310 Black
		Step Two: Backstitch (one strand)
227		701 Christmas Green-lt. (stems)
403		310 Black (all else)
		Step Three: French Knots (one strand)
403	●	310 Black
		Step Four: Lazy Daisy Stitch (one strand)
227	⬭	701 Christmas Green-lt.
		Step Five: Beadwork
	∴	Red
	▲	Red

Stitch Count: 96 x 102

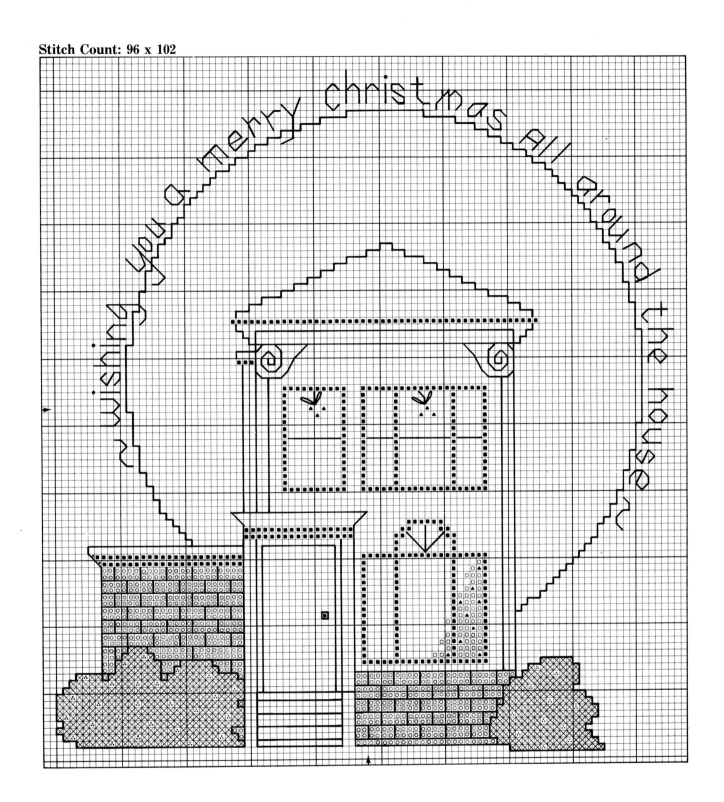

Christmas Heralds

Angels and shepherds proclaim the Christmas season today just as they did the very first Christmas. This pair of heralds was stitched on perforated paper and then sandwiched between two pieces of glass. Ribbons were glued to the matting, and then the matting was put over the glass and held in place by the frame.

SAMPLE

Stitched on perforated paper 15, the finished design size is 3¾" x 3⅛".

Use one 9" x 12" sheet of perforated paper. Finished design sizes using fabrics are Aida 11—5⅛" x 4¼"; Aida 14—4⅛" x 3⅜"; Aida 18—3⅛" x 2⅝"; Hardanger 22—2⅝" x 2⅛".

Shepherd

SUSAN BATES		DMC (used for sample)

Step One: Cross-stitch (three strands)

849	·	927 Grey Green-med.
869	‖	3042 Antique Violet-lt.
101	△	327 Antique Violet-dk.
44	●	814 Garnet-dk.

901	–	680 Old Gold-dk.
898	✕	611 Drab Brown-dk.
189	■	991 Aquamarine-dk.
401	▼	413 Pewter Grey-dk.
	◣	Gold Metallic (one strand)

Step Two: Backstitch (two strands)

101		327 Antique Violet-dk. (lettering)
44		814 Garnet-dk. (hat)
401		413 Pewter Grey-dk. (shoes)

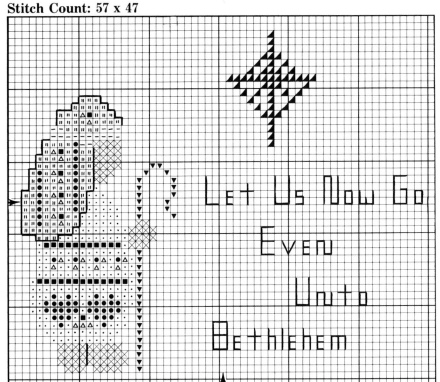

Let Us Now Go

Even

Unto

Bethlehem

Stitch Count: 46 x 57

I Bring You

Good Tidings Of

Great Joy

Angel

SUSAN BATES		DMC (used for sample)

Step One: Cross-stitch (three strands)

890	◢	729	Old Gold-med.
832	·	612	Drab Brown-med.
969	╱	316	Antique Mauve-med.
72	–	902	Garnet-vy. dk.
876	✕	502	Blue Green
101	o	327	Antique Violet-dk.
149	■	311	Navy Blue-med.

Step Two: Backstitch (two strands)

| 72 | | 902 | Garnet-vy. dk. |

123

Nativity Scene

Delicate colors and skillful shading complement the little angels and lambs gathered together in this cross-stitch Nativity scene.

SAMPLE

Stitched on white Linen 32 over two threads, the finished design size is 4⅜″ x 6¼″. The fabric was cut 10″ x 12″. Finished design sizes using other fabrics are Aida 11—6⅜″ x 9⅛″; Aida 14—5″ x 7¼″; Aida 18—3⅞″ x 5⅝″; Hardanger 22—3⅛″ x 4⅝″.

SUSAN BATES			DMC (used for sample)

Step One: Cross-stitch (two strands)

1			White
301			744 Yellow-pale
778			754 Peach Flesh-lt.
8			353 Peach Flesh
10			352 Coral-lt.
893			224 Shell Pink-lt.
969			316 Antique Mauve-med.
970			315 Antique Mauve-dk.
920			932 Antique Blue-lt.
215			368 Pistachio Green-lt.
216			367 Pistachio Green-dk.
886			677 Old Gold-vy. lt.
891			676 Old Gold-lt.
362			437 Tan-lt.
309			435 Brown-vy. lt.
379			840 Beige Brown-med.
380			839 Beige Brown-dk.
397			762 Pearl Grey-vy. lt.
399			452 Shell Grey-med.

Step Two: Filet Cross-stitch (one strand)

778		754 Peach Flesh-lt.
968		778 Antique Mauve-lt.
969		316 Antique Mauve-med.
869		3042 Antique Violet-lt.
871		3041 Antique Violet-med.
920		932 Antique Blue-lt.
167		598 Turquoise-lt.
875		503 Blue Green-med.
886		677 Old Gold-vy. lt.

Step Three: Backstitch (one strand)

399		452 Shell Grey-med. (around window panes)
401		844 Beaver Grey-ultra dk. (all else)

Stitch Count: 70 x 101

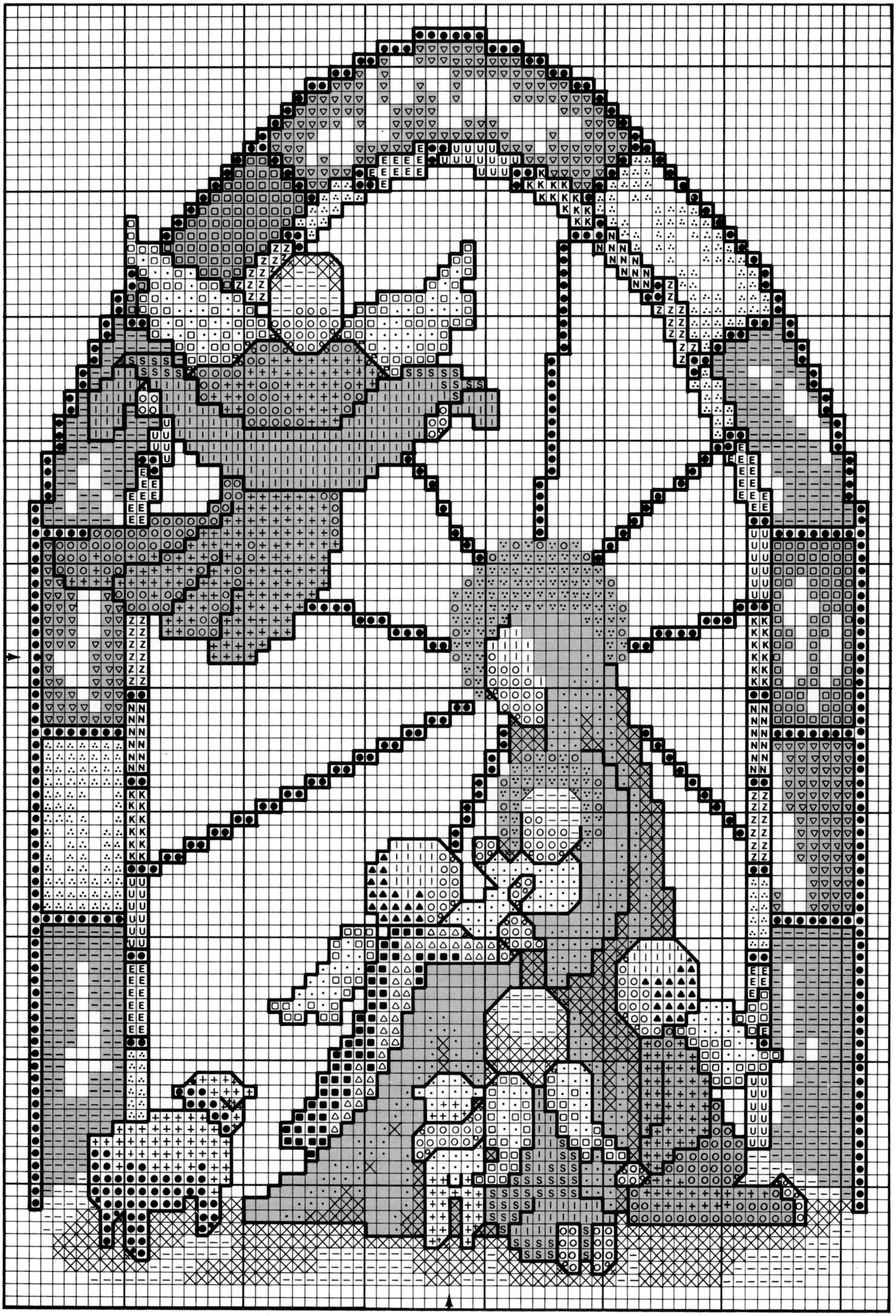

SUSAN BATES	DMC (used for sample)	

Step One: Cross-stitch (two strands)

1	·	White
386	+	746 Off-White
301	○ /	744 Yellow-pale
297	△	743 Yellow-med.
297	∵	743 Yellow-med. (bead sewn over cross-stitch)
778	─ /	948 Peach Flesh-vy. lt.
8	● /	761 Salmon-lt.
27	U	899 Rose-med.
27	A	899 Rose-med. (bead sewn over cross-stitch)
44	□ /	816 Garnet
44	Z	816 Garnet (bead sewn over cross-stitch)
104		210 Lavender-med. (bead sewn over cross-stitch)
869	E	3042 Antique Violet-lt.
120	· /	794 Cornflower Blue-lt.
120	N	794 Cornflower Blue-lt. (bead sewn over cross-stitch)
121	+	793 Cornflower Blue-med.
900	I	928 Grey Green-lt.
208	X	563 Jade-lt.
208	S	563 Jade-lt. (bead sewn over cross-stitch)
212	▼	561 Jade-vy. dk.
886	i	3047 Yellow Beige-lt.
887	X	3046 Yellow Beige-med.
373	●	3045 Yellow Beige-dk.
309	∵	781 Topaz-dk.
310	○	780 Topaz-vy. dk.
381	■	938 Coffee Brown-ultra dk.
397	△	762 Pearl Grey-vy. lt.
	▽	Gold Metallic

Step Two: Backstitch (one strand)

212		561 Jade-vy. dk. (poem and flower stems)
381		938 Coffee Brown-ultra dk. (all else)

Step Three: French Knots (one strand)

212	●	561 Jade-vy. dk.

Step Four: Beadwork (sewn over cross-stitch)

	∵	Pale Yellow
	A	Pink
	Z	Red
	─	Lavender
	N	Blue
	S	Green

Fairy Tale

A fairy-tale princess, encircled by a garland of flowers, pipes her Christmas greeting for all to hear.

SAMPLE

Stitched on white Linen 32 over two threads, the finished design size is 6¾" x 10⅝". The fabric was cut 13" x 17". Finished design sizes using other fabrics are Aida 11—10" x 15½"; Aida 14—7⅞" x 12⅛"; Aida 18—6⅛" x 9⅜"; Hardanger 22—5" x 7⅝".

Stitch Count: 88 x 73

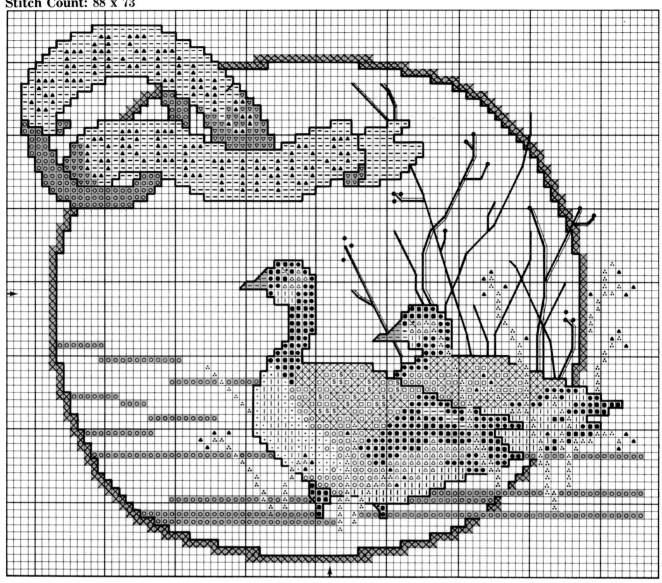

Season's Greetings

Decorate your favorite man's den or office for the holidays with this beautiful cross-stitch scene that combines season's greetings with nature's designs.

SAMPLE

Stitched on Fiddlers Lite 14, the finished design size is 6¼" x 5¼". The fabric was cut 15" x 15". Finished design sizes using other fabrics are Aida 11—8" x 6⅝"; Aida 14—6¼" x 5¼"; Aida 18—4⅞" x 4"; Hardanger 22—4" x 3⅜".

FINISHING OPTION

Using 1⅞ yards of ¹⁄₁₆"-wide red satin ribbon, tie bows and drape ribbon above and to the left side of the framed cross-stitch piece. Glue where necessary, to hold the curves and the bows in place (see photo).

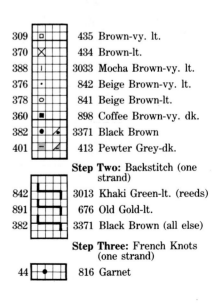

SUSAN BATES		DMC (used for sample)
		Step One: Cross-stitch (two strands)
926	△	Ecru
44	▲	816 Garnet
920	○	932 Antique Blue-lt.
842	∴	3013 Khaki Green-lt.
269	✕	936 Avocado Green-vy. dk.
891	−	676 Old Gold-lt.
890	▽	729 Old Gold-med.
362	s	437 Tan-lt.
309	▫	435 Brown-vy. lt.
370	✕	434 Brown-lt.
388	‖	3033 Mocha Brown-vy. lt.
376	·	842 Beige Brown-vy. lt.
378	○	841 Beige Brown-lt.
360	■	898 Coffee Brown-vy. dk.
382	● ⁄	3371 Black Brown
401	− ⁄	413 Pewter Grey-dk.

Step Two: Backstitch (one strand)

842		3013 Khaki Green-lt. (reeds)
891		676 Old Gold-lt.
382		3371 Black Brown (all else)

Step Three: French Knots (one strand)

44	●	816 Garnet

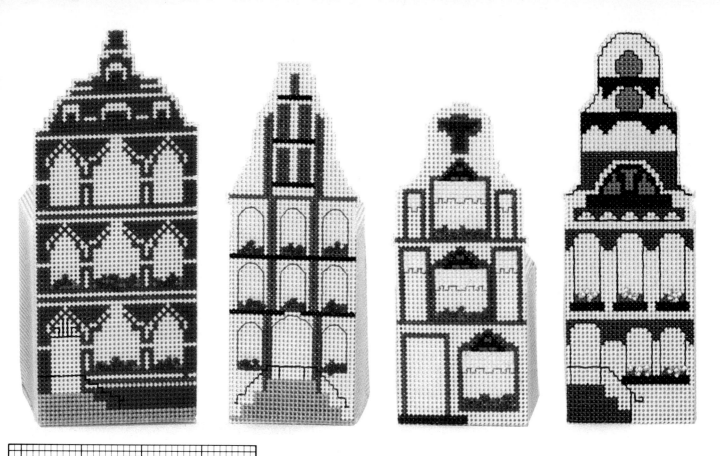

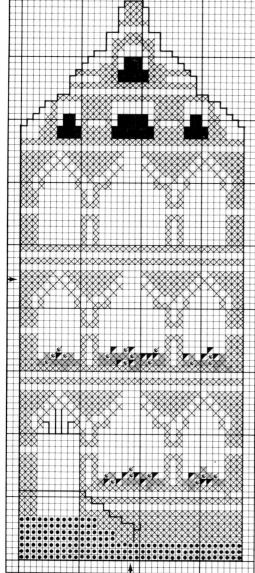

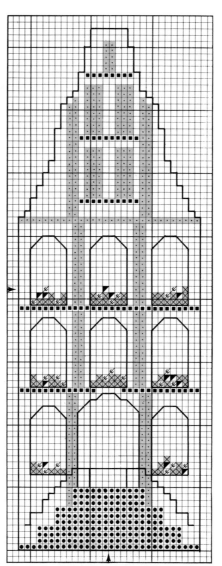

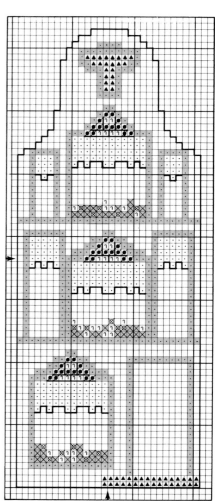

Row Houses

Patterned after streets in old Amsterdam, these quaint little row houses can be stitched on fabric or paper. Stitch the entire design on fabric and hang the finished piece, or stitch each house on perforated paper and make three-dimensional buildings. Group several or all of them to add a quaint touch to your mantel or buffet.

SAMPLE

Stitched on cream Aida 18, the finished design size of the framed picture is 16⅛″ x 5″. The fabric was cut 23″ x 12″. Cross-stitching was done with two strands of floss and backstitching with one strand. Finished design sizes using other fabrics are Aida 11—26½″ x 8⅛″; Aida 14—20¾″ x 6⅜″; Hardanger 22—13¼″ x 4⅛″.

SAMPLE

Stitched on cream perforated paper 15, the finished design sizes are small house—2″ x 4⅞″; medium house—2″ x 6″; large house—2½″ x 5⅞″. Use one 9″ x 12″ piece of perforated paper for each house. Trace the pattern for the house onto the paper and center the design in the front panel.

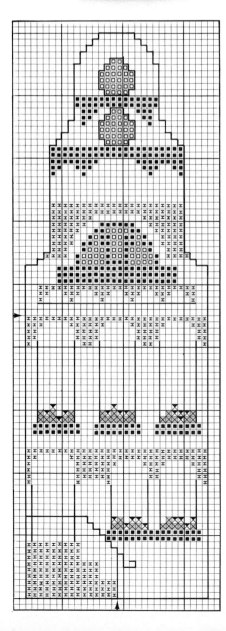

SUSAN BATES		DMC (used for sample)
		Step One: Cross-stitch (three strands for perforated paper)
386	·	746 Off-White
74	∴	3354 Dusty Rose-lt.
74	⊠	3354 Dusty Rose-lt. (bead over cross-stitch)
42	Γ	3350 Dusty Rose-vy. dk.
42	⊠	3350 Dusty Rose-vy. dk. (bead over cross-stitch)
897	A	221 Shell Pink-dk.
897	■	221 Shell Pink-dk. (bead over cross-stitch)
19	◥	817 Coral Red-vy. dk. (bead over cross-stitch)
19	⌀	817 Coral Red-vy. dk.
44	○	815 Garnet-med. (bead over cross-stitch)
244	⊠	987 Forest Green-dk.
779	⊡	926 Grey Green-dk.
851	⫴	924 Grey Green-vy. dk.
149	◣	311 Navy Blue-med.
5968	⊠	355 Terra Cotta-dk.
882		407 Sportsman Flesh-dk.
936	·	632 Dark Flesh
380	■	839 Beige Brown-dk.
382	▲	3021 Brown Grey-dk.
399	●	318 Steel Grey-lt.
403	■	310 Black

		Step Two: Backstitch (one strand)
851		924 Grey Green-vy. dk. (inside house #8)
882		407 Sportsman Flesh-dk. (inside house #4)
936		632 Dark Flesh (inside houses #4 and #9)
382		3021 Brown Grey-dk. (inside house #2)
403		310 Black (all else)

Step Three: Beadwork

⊠	Light Pink
⊠	Dark Pink
■	Dark Red
⌀	Light Red
○	Dark Red

continued **131**

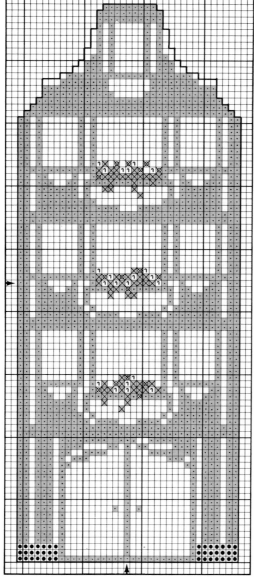

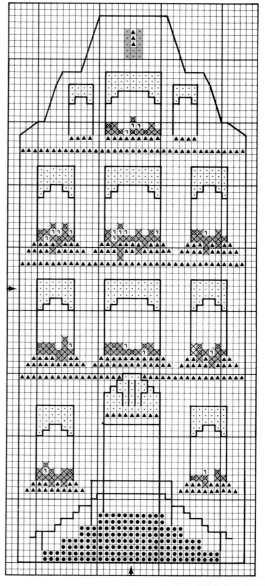

MATERIALS

Completed cross-stitch on cream
  perforated paper
One manila file folder
Rubber cement
Tracing paper for pattern

DIRECTIONS

1. Transfer the pattern for house, including all information.

2. Center the front panel of the pattern over the wrong side of the design, aligning the bottom edge of the design with the fold line. Trace the pattern.

3. Cut out the house one space from the stitched design and pencil lines; do not cut on the fold lines.

4. Trace and cut out the front panel of the house from the manila folder.

5. Glue the manila front panel to the wrong side of the perforated paper front panel for support. Trim the top edges to match.

6. Fold on fold lines. Glue tabs to sides in alphabetical sequence.

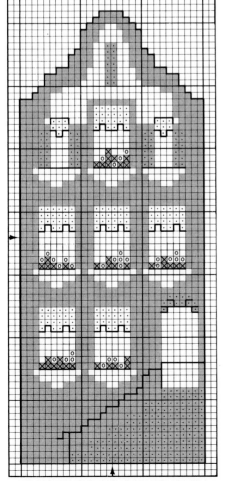

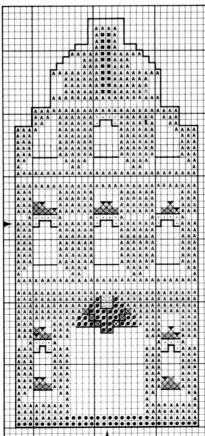

133

One square equals one inch.

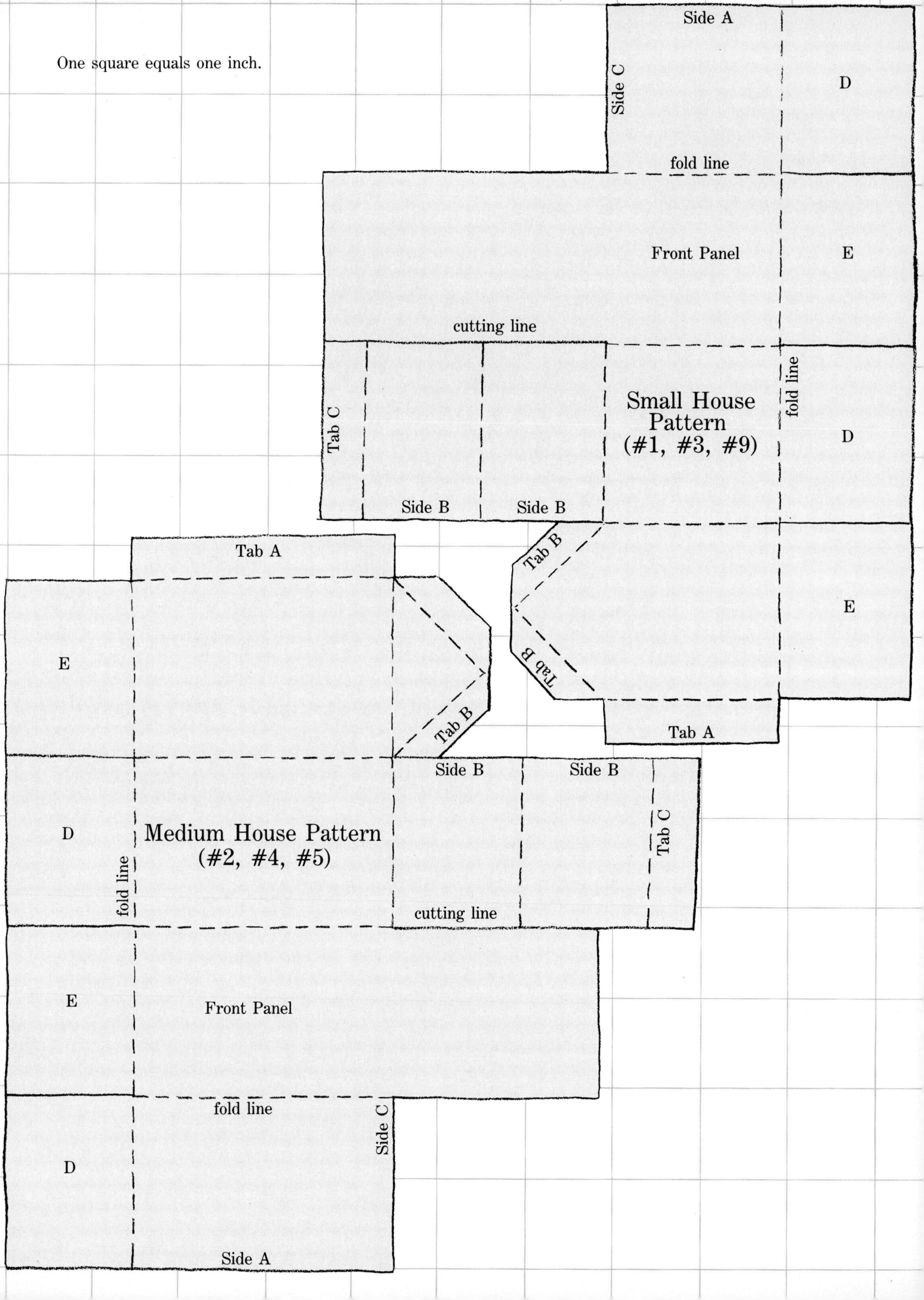

Side A

Side C

D

fold line

Front Panel

E

cutting line

Tab C

fold line

Small House
Pattern
(#1, #3, #9)

D

Side B   Side B

Tab B

E

Tab B

Tab B

Tab A

Tab A

E

Side B   Side B

D

Tab C

Medium House Pattern
(#2, #4, #5)

fold line

E

Front Panel

cutting line

Side C

fold line

D

Side A

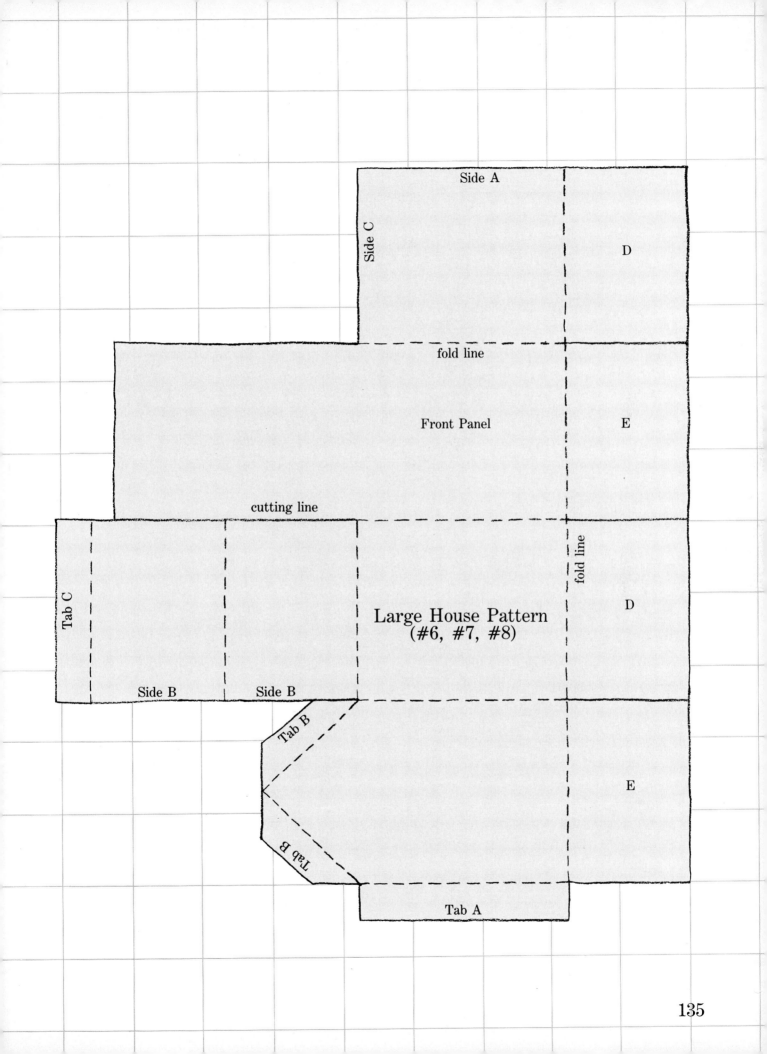

Side A

Side C

D

fold line

Front Panel

E

cutting line

Tab C

Side B

Side B

**Large House Pattern
(#6, #7, #8)**

fold line

D

Tab B

Tab B

E

Tab A

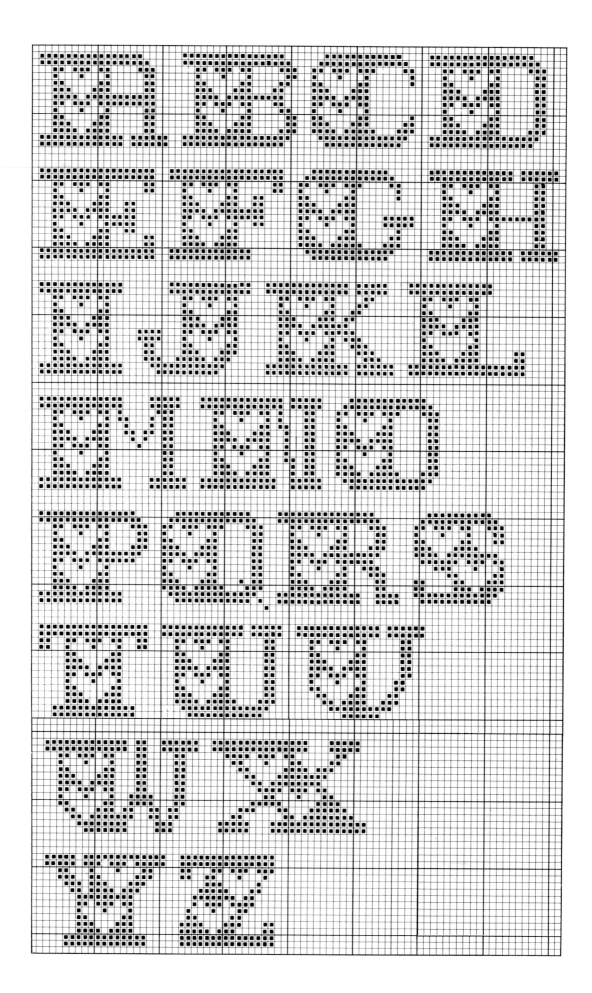

136

Appendix

Heart Alphabet

Personalize the stockings on page 8, the Monogrammed Sachets on page 15 and the Wine Bags on page 103 with this Heart Alphabet.

Cross-stitch

Fabrics: Most fabrics used in this book are even-weave fabrics made especially for cross-stitch and are available in needlework departments or shops. Fabrics used for the models in the photographs are identified in the sample information by color, name, and thread count per inch.

Finished Design Size: To determine the finished size of a design, divide the stitch count by the threads per inch of the fabric. When designs are stitched over two threads, divide the stitch count by half of the threads per inch.

Needles: Use a blunt tapestry needle that slips easily through the holes and does not pierce the fabric. With fabric that has eleven or fewer threads per inch, use needle size 24; with fourteen threads per inch, use needle size 24 or 26; with eighteen threads or more per inch, use needle size 26.

Preparing Fabric: Cut the fabric 3″ larger on all sides than the finished design size, or cut as indicated in sample information. To keep the fabric from fraying, whipstitch or machine-zigzag the raw edges.

Hoop or Frame: Select a hoop or stretcher bars large enough to hold the entire design. Place a screw or the clamp of the hoop in a 10 o'clock

position (or 2 o'clock, if you are left handed) to keep from catching the thread.

Floss: Cut the floss into 18″ lengths. For best coverage, run the floss over a damp sponge and separate all six strands. Put back together the number of strands recommended for use in sample information. If the floss becomes twisted while stitching, drop the needle and allow the floss to unwind. The floss will cover best when lying flat.

Centering Design: Find the center of the fabric by folding it from top to bottom and again from left to right. Place a pin in the point of the fold to mark the center. Locate the center of the graph by following the vertical and horizontal arrows. Begin stitching at the center point of the graph and fabric. Each square on the graph represents one complete cross-stitch. Unless indicated otherwise in sample information, each stitch is over one unit of thread.

Securing Floss: Never knot floss unless working on clothing. Hold 1″ of thread behind the fabric and secure it with the first few stitches. To secure the thread when finishing, run it under four or more stitches on the back of the design.

Reading Graphs: To help distinguish the colors in designs, shade the graphs with colored pencils.

Backstitching: Complete all cross-stitches before working backstitches or accent stitches. When backstitching, use the number of strands indicated in the code or one strand fewer than was used for cross-stitching.

Stitching Method: Use a "push and pull" method for the smoothest stitch. Push the needle straight down and completely through the fabric before pulling it up.

Carrying Floss: Do not carry floss more than ½″ between stitched areas, because loose threads, especially dark ones, will show through the fabric. Run the floss under worked stitches on the back when possible.

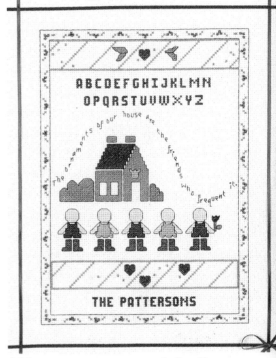

Add your own name and family members to make this Family Sampler uniquely yours (see graph, page 55).

Cleaning Completed Work: After making sure fabric and floss are colorfast, briefly soak the completed work in cold water. If it is soiled, wash it gently in mild soap. Roll the work in a towel to remove excess water; do not wring. Place the work face down on a dry, lightweight towel and press it with a warm iron until it is dry.

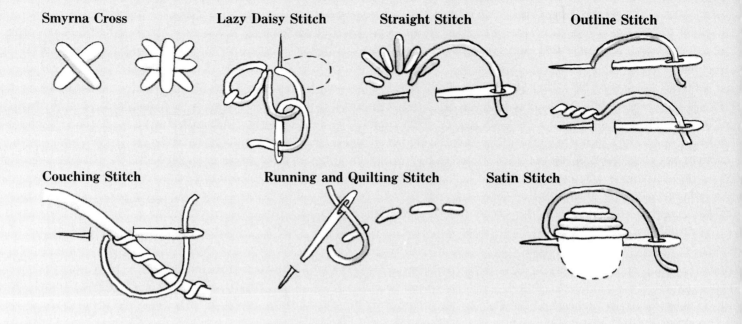

Smyrna Cross   **Lazy Daisy Stitch**   **Straight Stitch**   **Outline Stitch**

Couching Stitch   **Running and Quilting Stitch**   **Satin Stitch**

Stitches

Cross-Stitch: Bring the needle and thread up at A, down at B, up at C, and down again at D (Diagram 1). For rows, stitch all the way across so that floss is angled from the lower left to upper right; then return (Diagram 2). *All stitches must lie in the same direction.*

Diagram 1

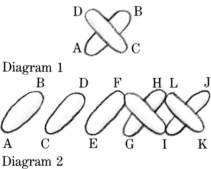

Diagram 2

Half-Cross: Indicated on graph by a slanted line with the color symbol beside it (Diagram 3). Make the longer stitch in the direction of the slanted line.

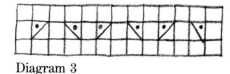

Diagram 3

The stitch actually fits three-fourths of the area (Diagram 4). Bring the needle and thread up at A and down at B, up at C and down at D.

 Diagram 4

In cases where two colors meet, the graph will be similar to Diagram 5. The stitched area will look like Diagram 6.

Diagram 5   **Diagram 6**

Backstitch: Work from left to right with one strand of floss (unless designated otherwise in the code). Bring the needle and thread up at A, down at B, and up again at C. Going back down at A, continue to stitch in this manner (Diagram 7).

Diagram 7

Beadwork: Attach beads to fabric with a half-cross, lower left to upper right. Secure the beads by returning the thread through the beads, lower right to upper left. Complete an entire row of half-crosses before returning to secure all the beads.

Slipstitch: Insert needle at A, slide it through the folded edge of the fabric for about 1/8" to 1/4" and bring it out at B. Directly below B, take a small stitch through the second piece of fabric.

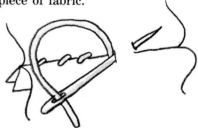

Whipstitch: With pieces pinned together, whipstitch over the edge with double strands of matching thread. Stitches should be spaced evenly, no more than 1/8" apart. Begin stitching with knot on inside.

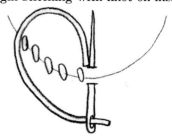

Sewing Hints

Circle Pattern Instructions: To make a circle pattern, tie a string around a pencil. Measure half the diameter of desired circle from the pencil and tie a knot in string at that point. Place the knot in the center of the paper and hold it with your thumb. Move the pencil in a circle at the end of the string. Check the measurements of the finished circle.

Basting: Basting stitches are done by hand, to temporarily hold layers of fabric and fleece or batting in a particular position. Remove the stitches once the project is complete. Basting stitches are usually sewn with a contrasting color of thread that is easy to see but will not leave marks. (Some dark colors leave a trail.)

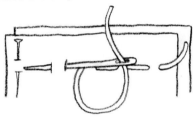

Bias Strips: Bias strips are used for ruffles, binding, or cording. To cut bias, fold the fabric at a 45° angle to the grain of the fabric and crease. Cut on the crease. Cut additional strips the width indicated in instructions and parallel to the first cutting line. The ends of the bias strips should be on the grain of fabric. Place the right sides of the ends together and stitch with a ¼″ seam. Continue to piece the strips until they are the length that is indicated in instructions.

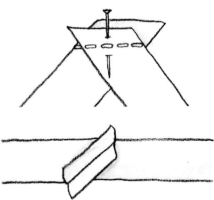

Topstitching: Topstitching is used as an accent on the top of the fabric. The stitching should be uniform, and it is usually parallel to a seam or part of the design.

Clipping Seams: Clipping seam allowances is necessary on all curves, points, and most corners so that the finished seam will lie flat. Clip into the seam allowance at even intervals, ¼″ to ½″ apart, being careful not to cut through the stitching.

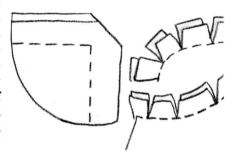

Cording (also called welting or piping): Piece bias strips together to equal the length needed for cording. Place the cord in the center of the wrong side of the strip and fold the fabric over it. Using a zipper foot, stitch close to the cord through both layers of fabric. Trim the seam allowance ¼″ from the stitching line.

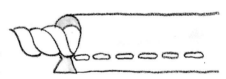

Gathers: Machine-stitch two parallel rows of long stitches ¼″ and ½″ from the edge of fabric (unless instructions say differently). Leave the ends of the thread 2″ or 3″ long. Pull the two bobbin threads and gather to fit the desired length. Long edges may need to be gathered from both ends. Disperse the fullness evenly and secure the threads in the seam by wrapping them around a pin in a figure eight.

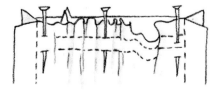

Designers

Pauline Asmus
Trice Boerens
Jo Buehler
Linda Calvert
Linda Durbano
Linda Hendrickson
Shelly James
Margaret Marti
Liz Mueller
Tina Richards
Doug Simmons
Julie Truman
Susan Wiseman
Terrece Woodruff

The Vanessa-Ann Collection Staff

Owners: Jo Buehler and Terrece Woodruff
Editor: Margaret Marti
Editor: Heather Hales
Art Director: Trice Boerens
Needlework Director: Nancy Whitley
Finishing Director: Susan Whitelock
Graphic Artist: Julie Truman
Copy Editor: Brenda Schussman
Graphing Director: Susan Jorgensen
Operations Manager: Karen Gardiner
Comptroller: Katie Pearce
Accounting Officer: Pam Randall
Office Manager: Barbara Milburn

We also wish to acknowledge the contributions of Carol McCafferty, Lori Ward and Scott Read.

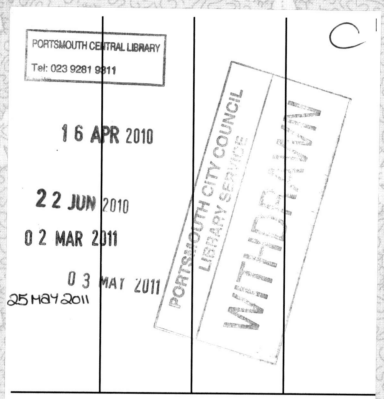